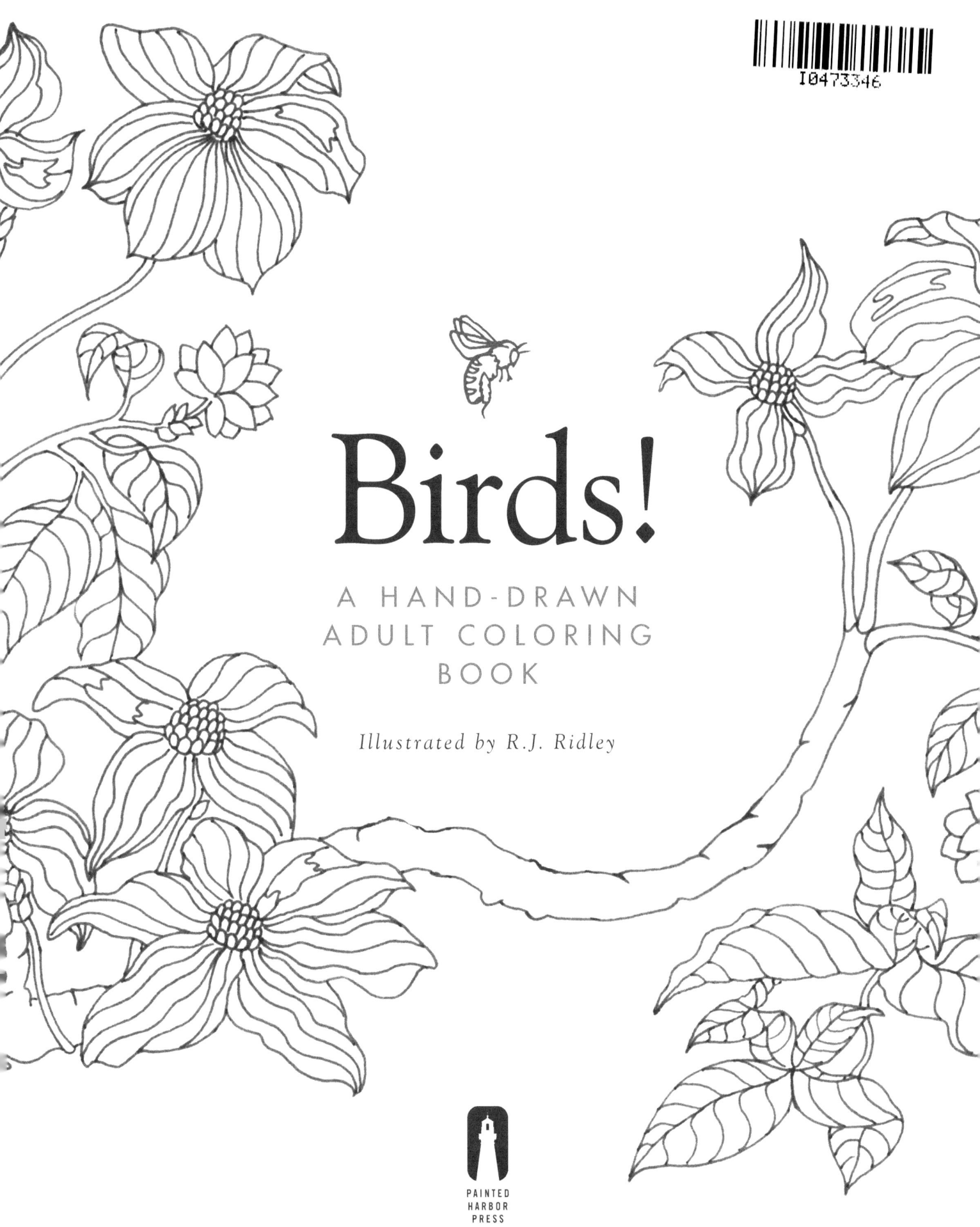

Birds!

A HAND-DRAWN ADULT COLORING BOOK

Illustrated by R.J. Ridley

PAINTED
HARBOR
PRESS

Artwork © 2015-2016 by R.J. Ridley
Cover design by James T. Egan of Bookfly Design

Printed in the United States of America

FIRST PRINTING: 2016

ISBN 978-0-9979805-0-9

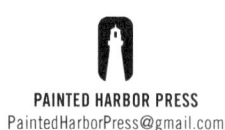

PAINTED HARBOR PRESS
PaintedHarborPress@gmail.com

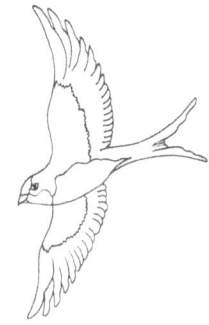

THIS BOOK features 28 original hand-drawn illustrations of birds from around the world in their natural habitats.

———————

THE COMMON AND SCIENTIFIC NAMES of each bird are printed on the back side of the page. Color according to the bird's real-life plumage, or create your own designs!

———————

A DUPLICATE COPY OF EACH DRAWING is included so you can experiment with different coloring techniques or share with a family member or friend.

———————

THE ILLUSTRATIONS are printed on one side of the page. We recommend placing a piece of cardboard or thick paper behind the page when coloring with markers or other wet mediums to avoid bleed-through.

ABOUT THE ILLUSTRATOR

R.J. RIDLEY is an artist, a wildlife biologist, and an avid birdwatcher. When she's not exploring the West observing and identifying birds, she can often be found with pencil and sketchbook in hand. Many of the illustrations in this book were originally drawn in the field.

Test Page

USE THIS PAGE TO TEST YOUR PENCILS, MARKERS,
OR OTHER COLORING MEDIUMS BEFORE GETTING STARTED.

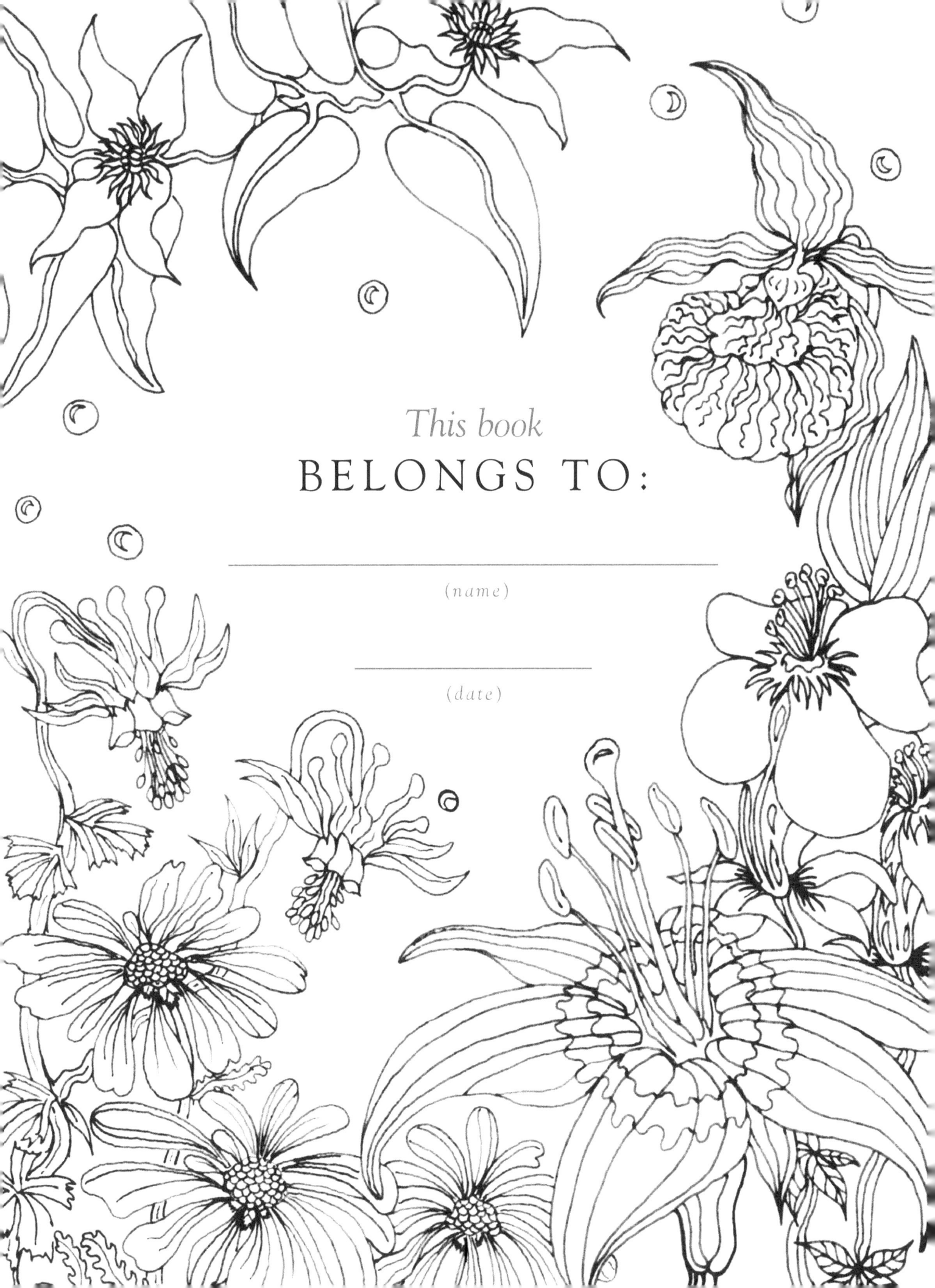

This book
BELONGS TO:

_____
(name)

_____
(date)

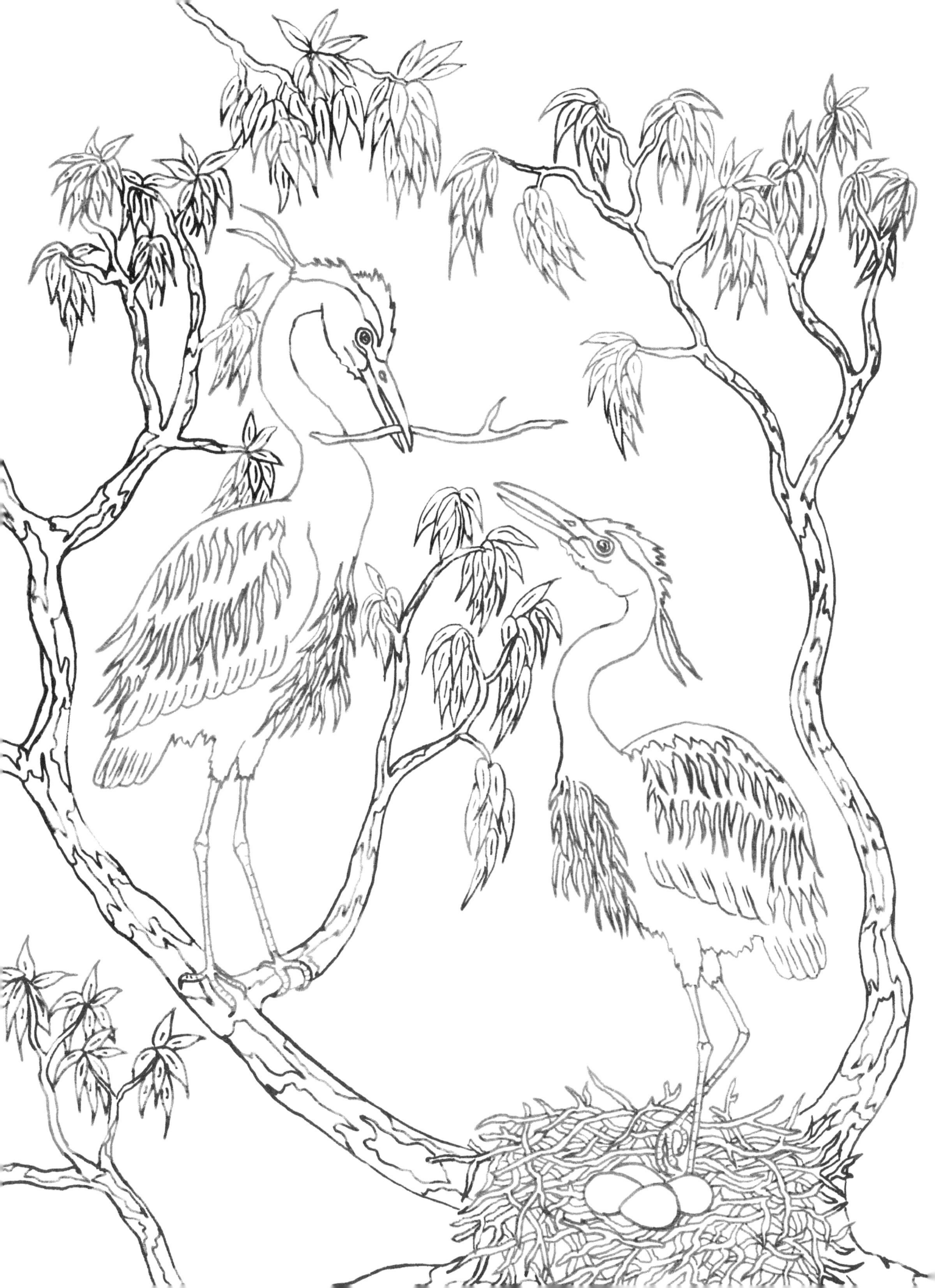

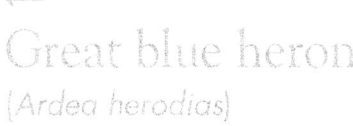

Great blue heron
(*Ardea herodias*)

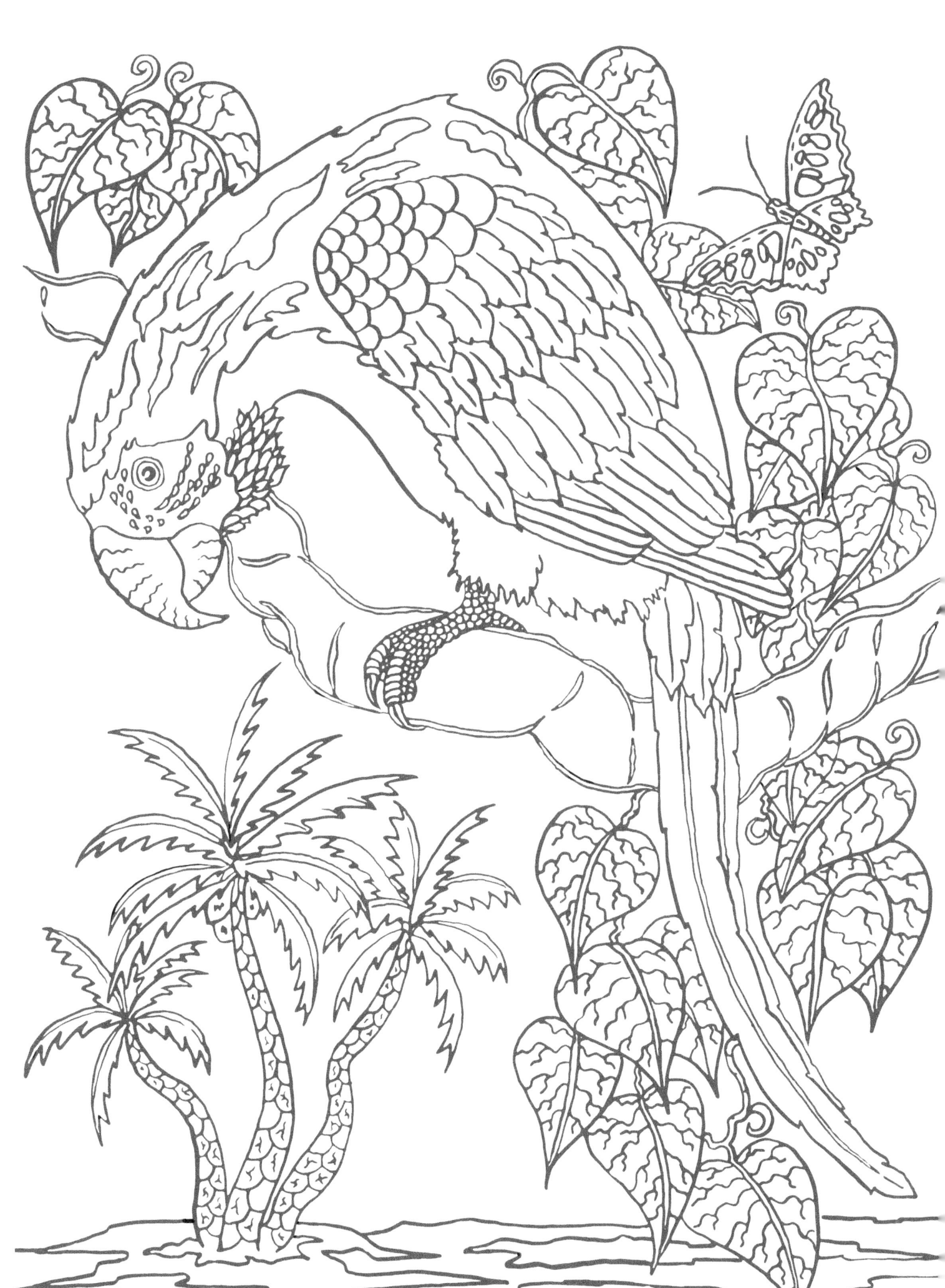

Blue and gold macaw
(*Ara ararauna*)

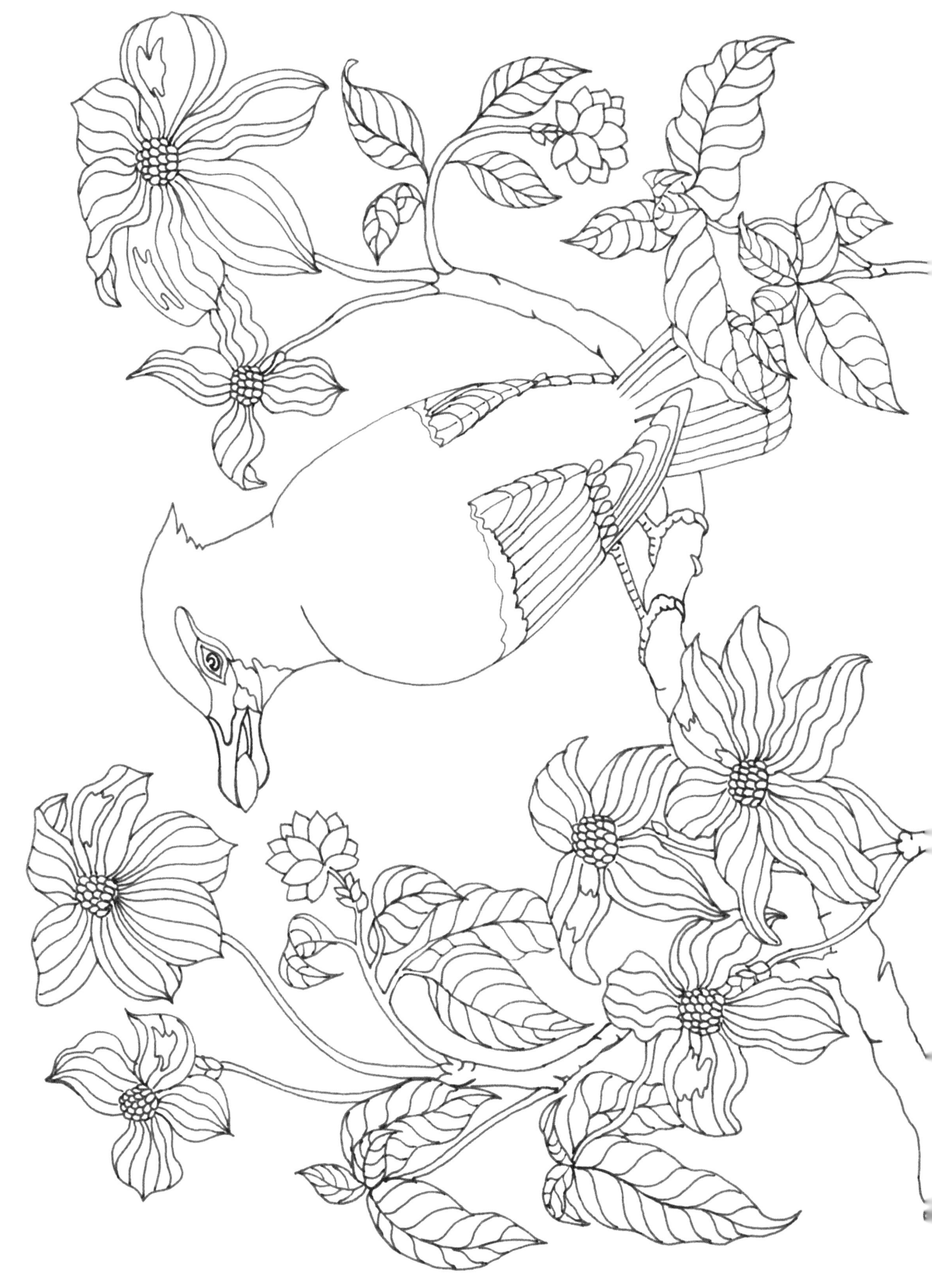

Bohemian waxwing
(*Bombycilla garrulus*)

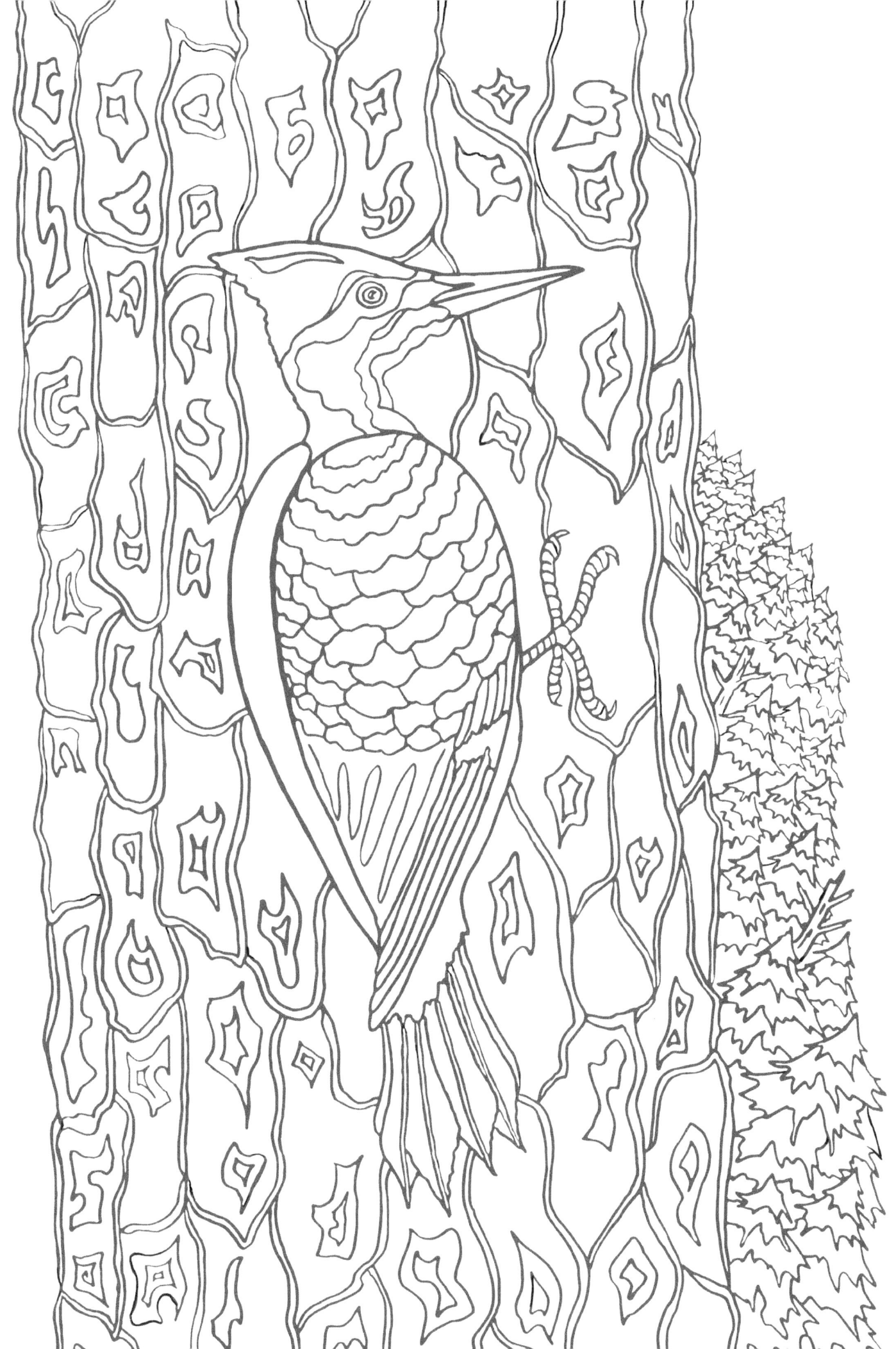

←

Pileated woodpecker
(Dryocopus pileatus)

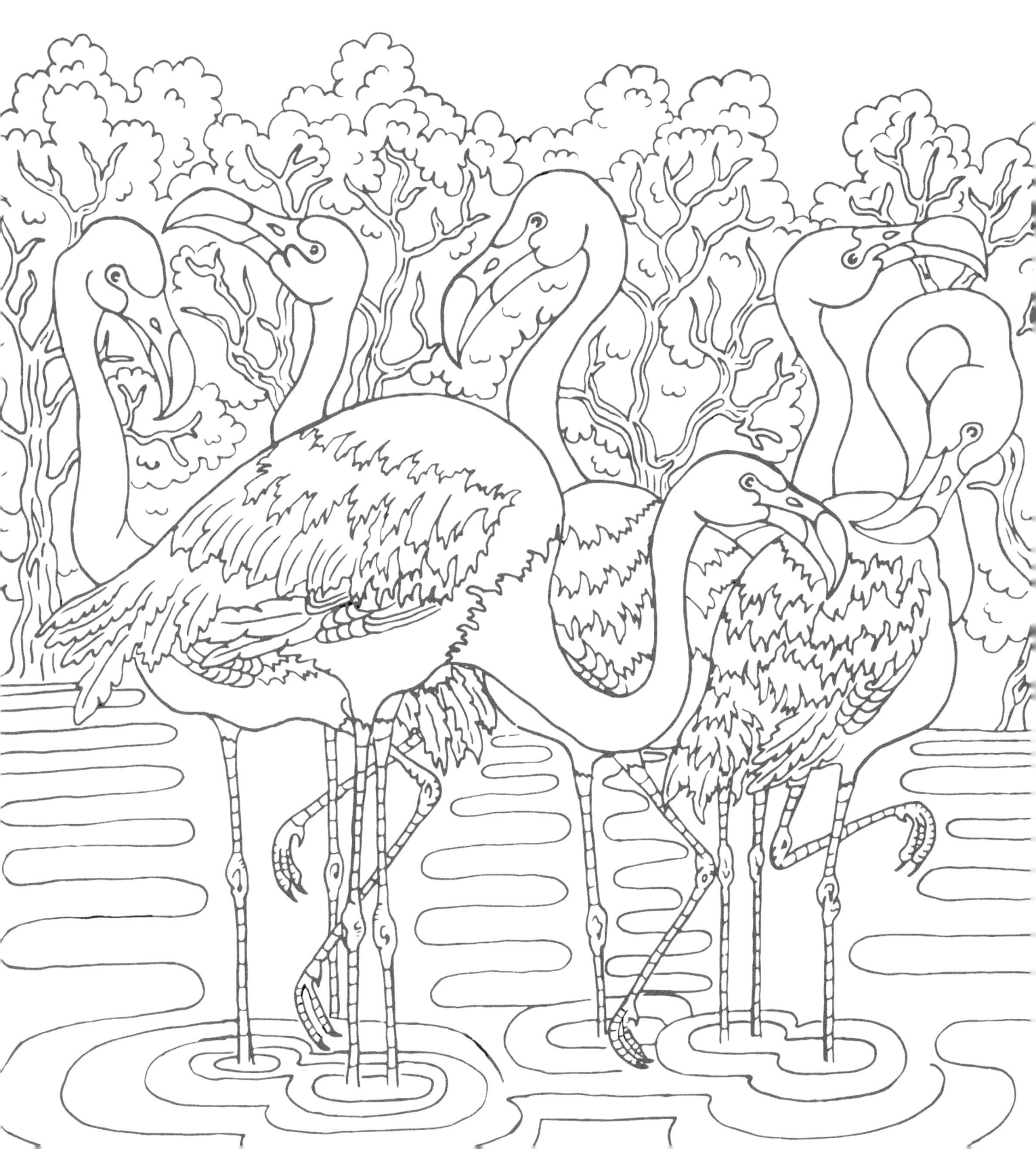

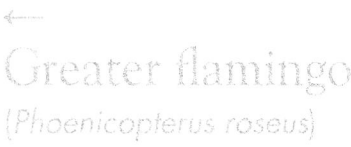

Greater flamingo
(Phoenicopterus roseus)

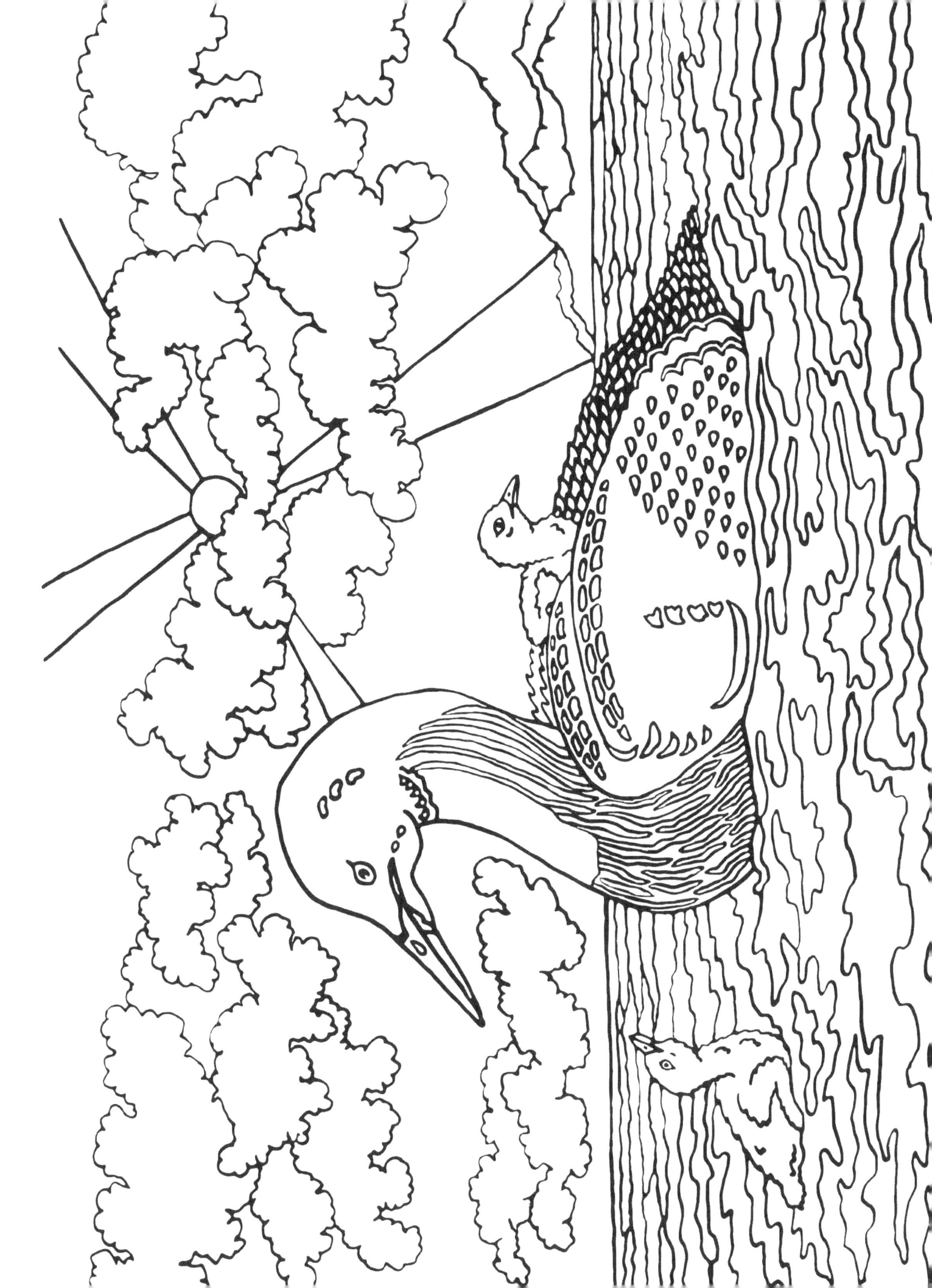

←

Pacific loon
(*Gavia pacifica*)

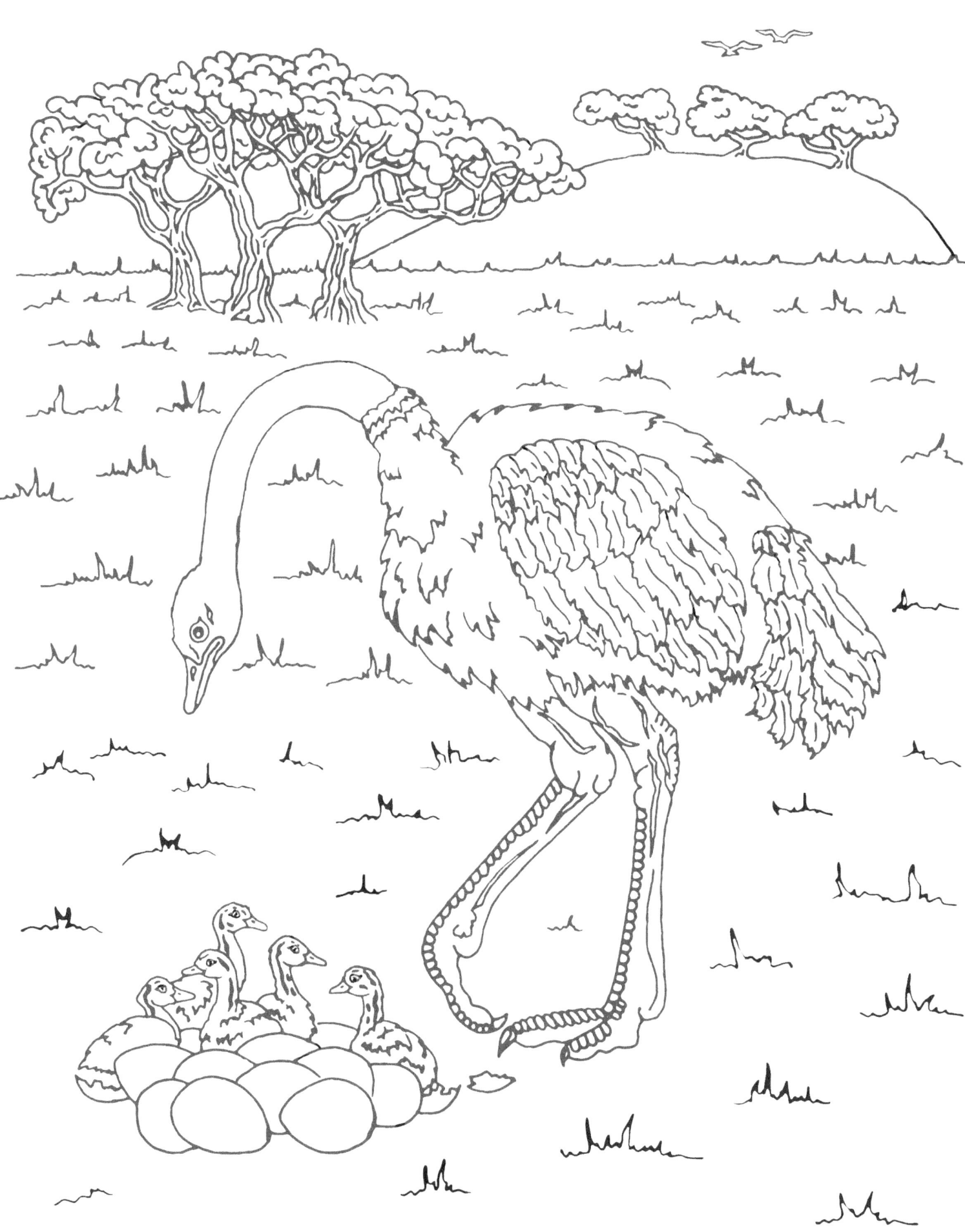

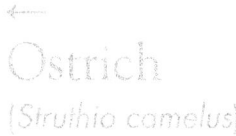

Ostrich
(Struthio camelus)

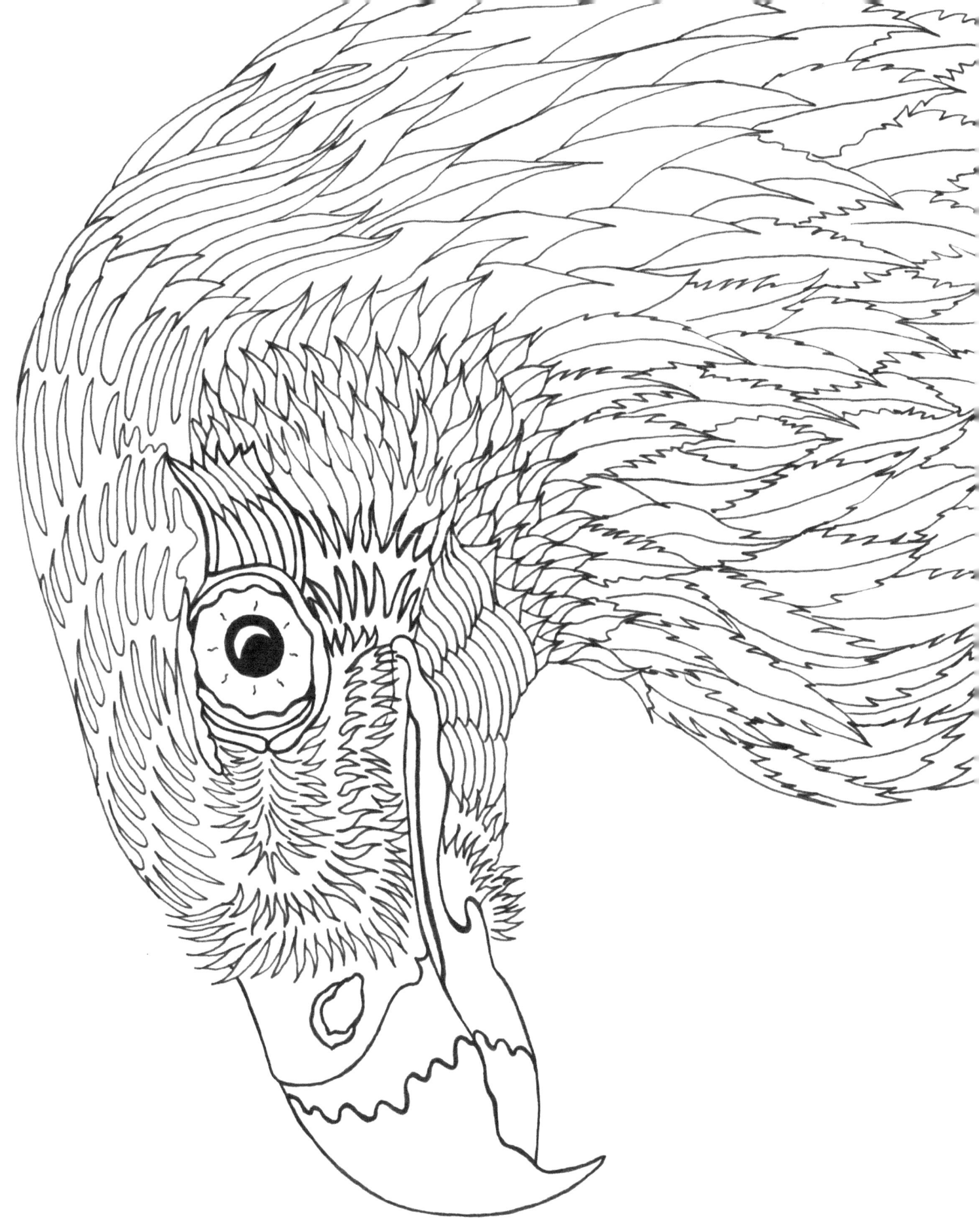

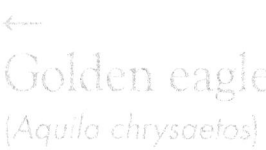

Golden eagle
(Aquila chrysaetos)

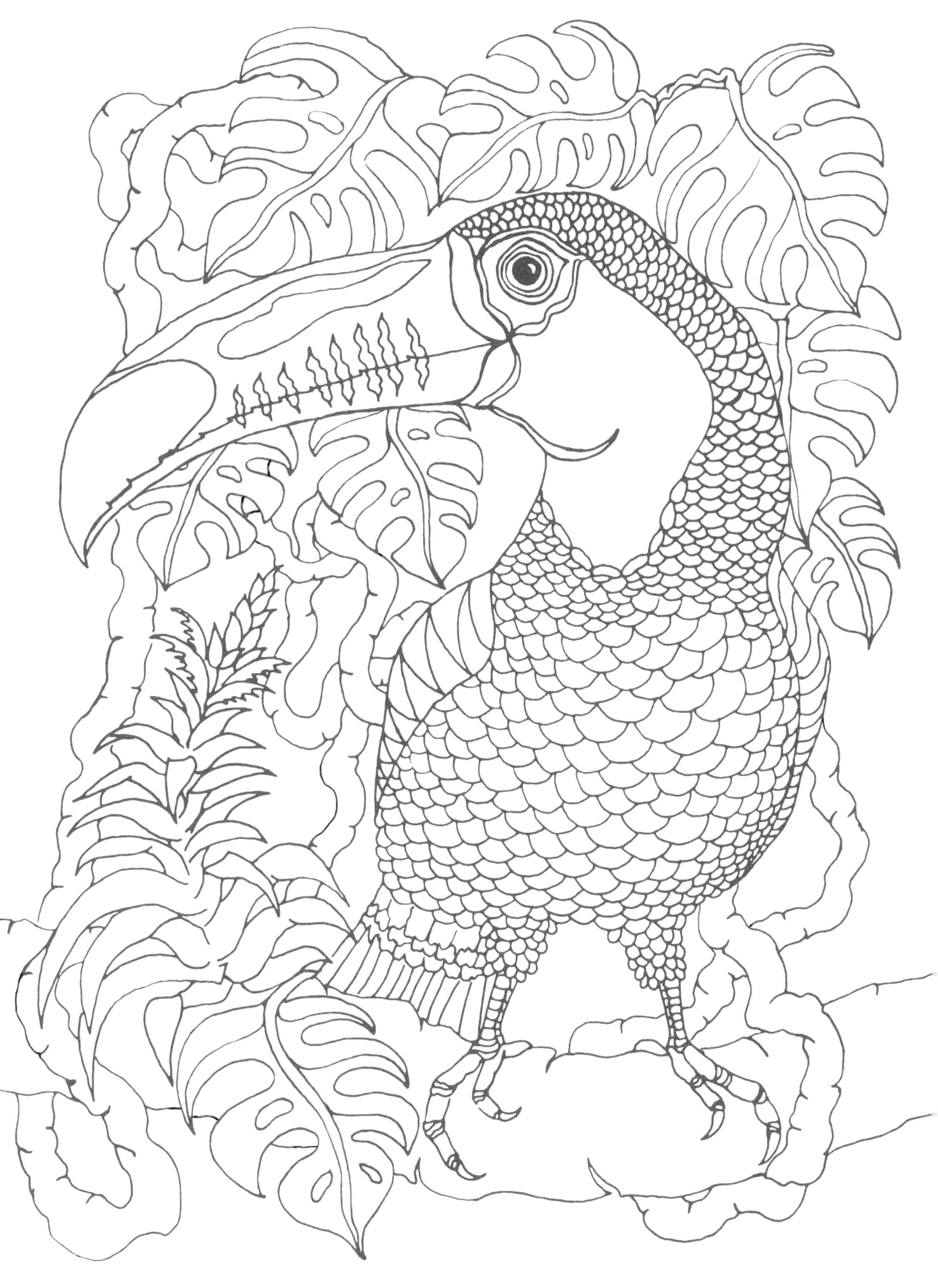

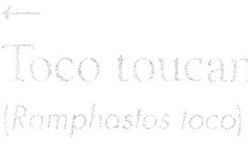

Toco toucan
(Ramphastos toco)

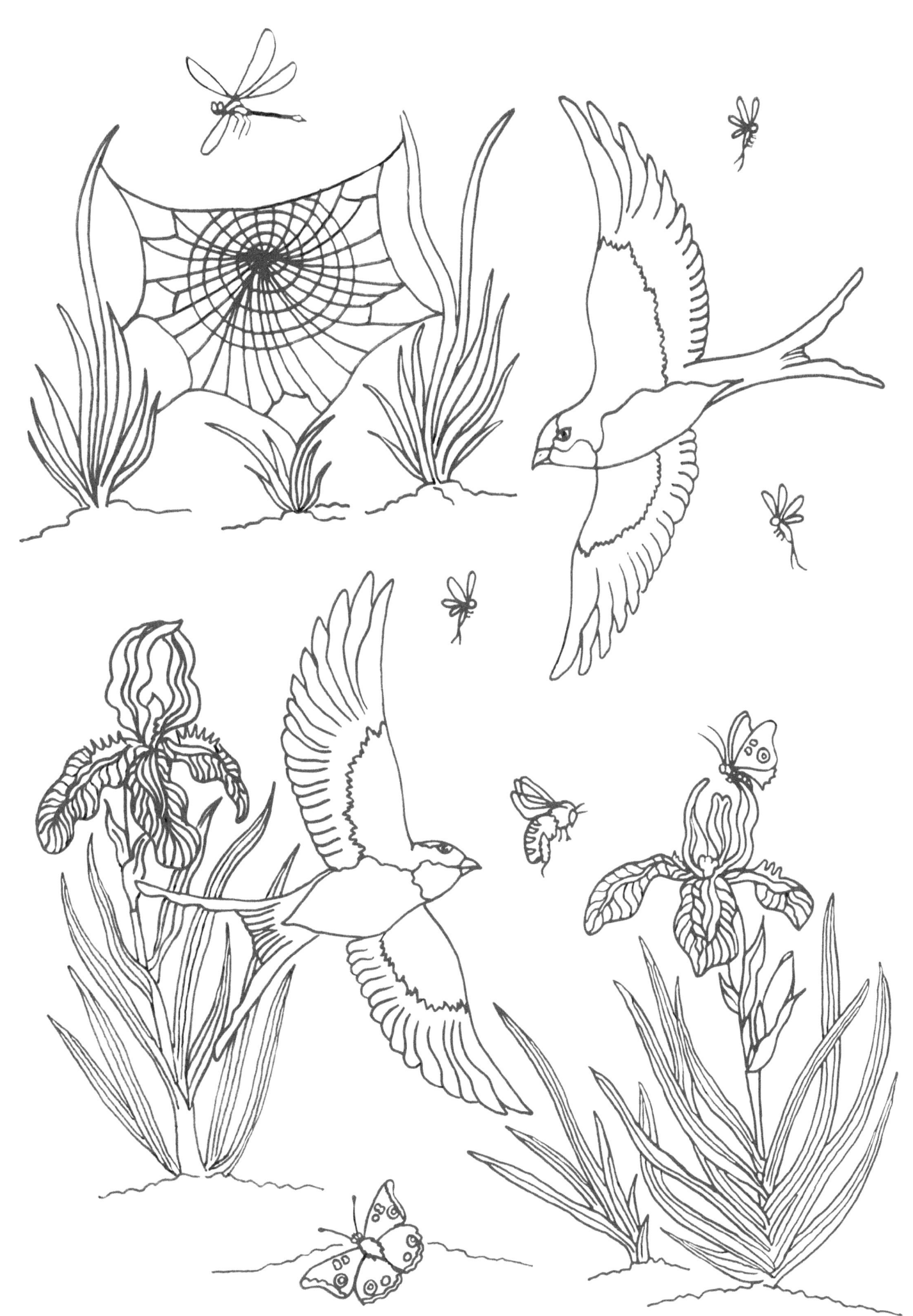

←·····

Barn swallows
(*Hirundo rustica*)

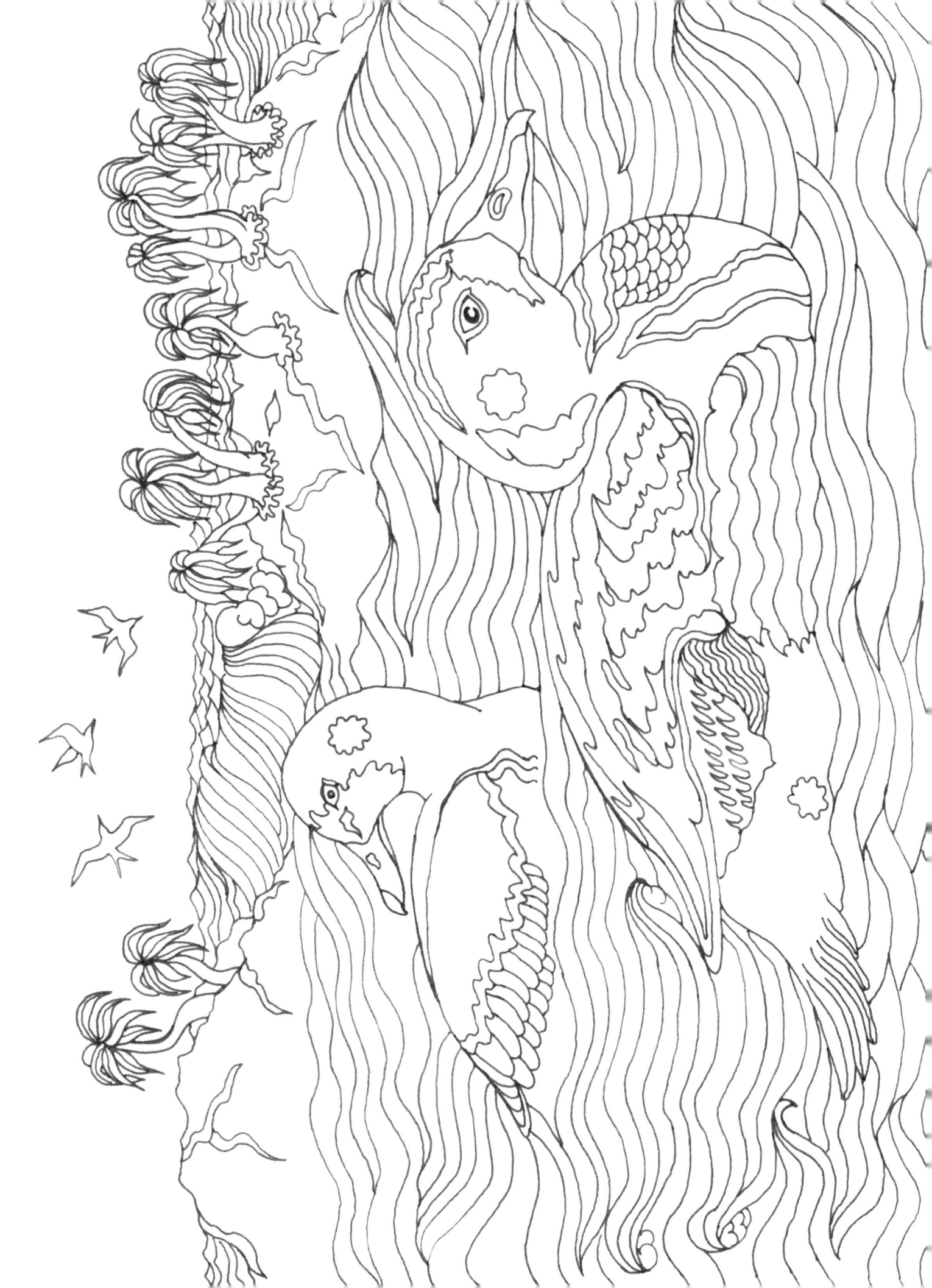

←

Harlequin duck
(*Histrionicus histrionicus*)

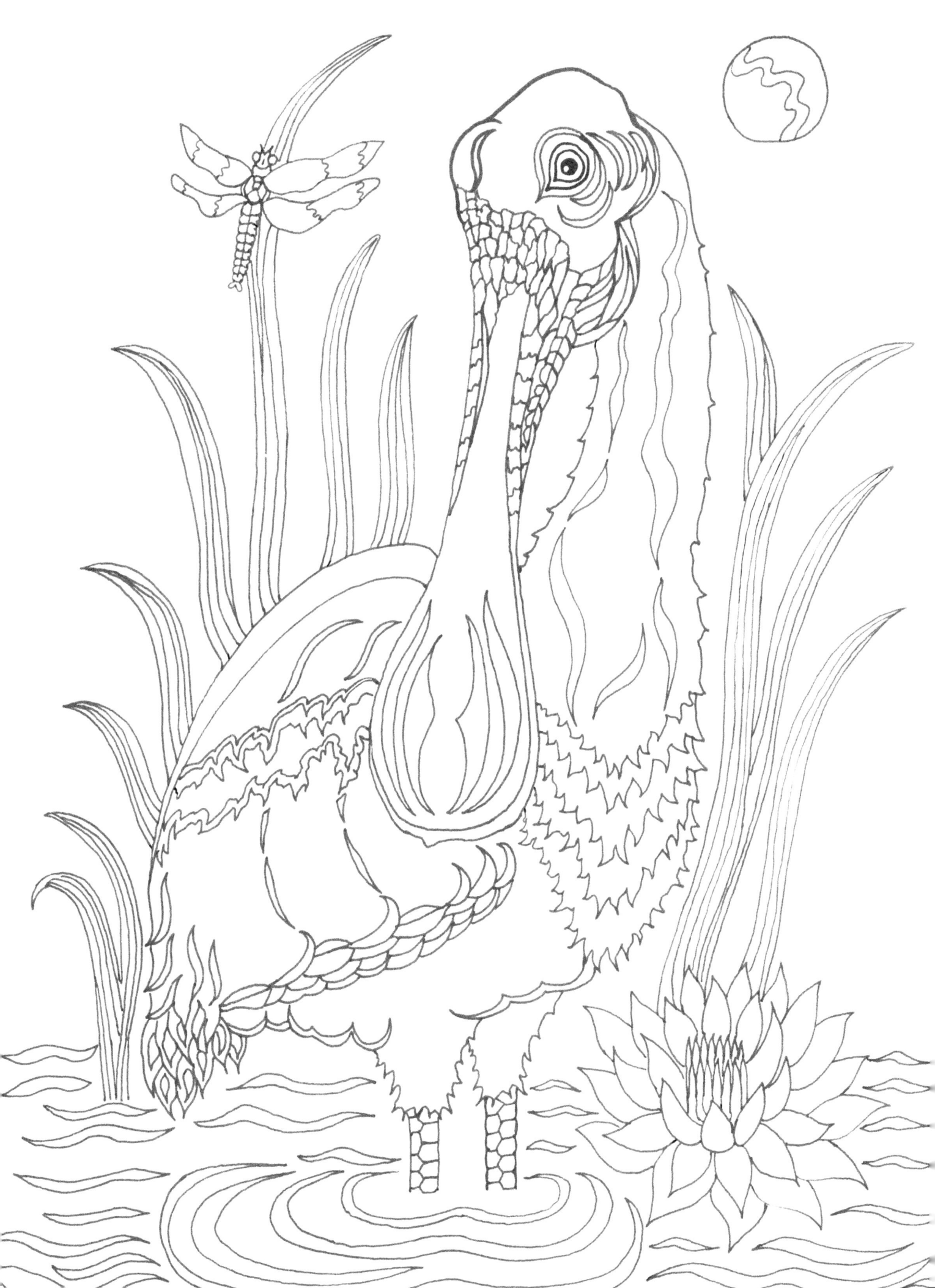

←

Roseate spoonbill
(*Platalea ajaja*)

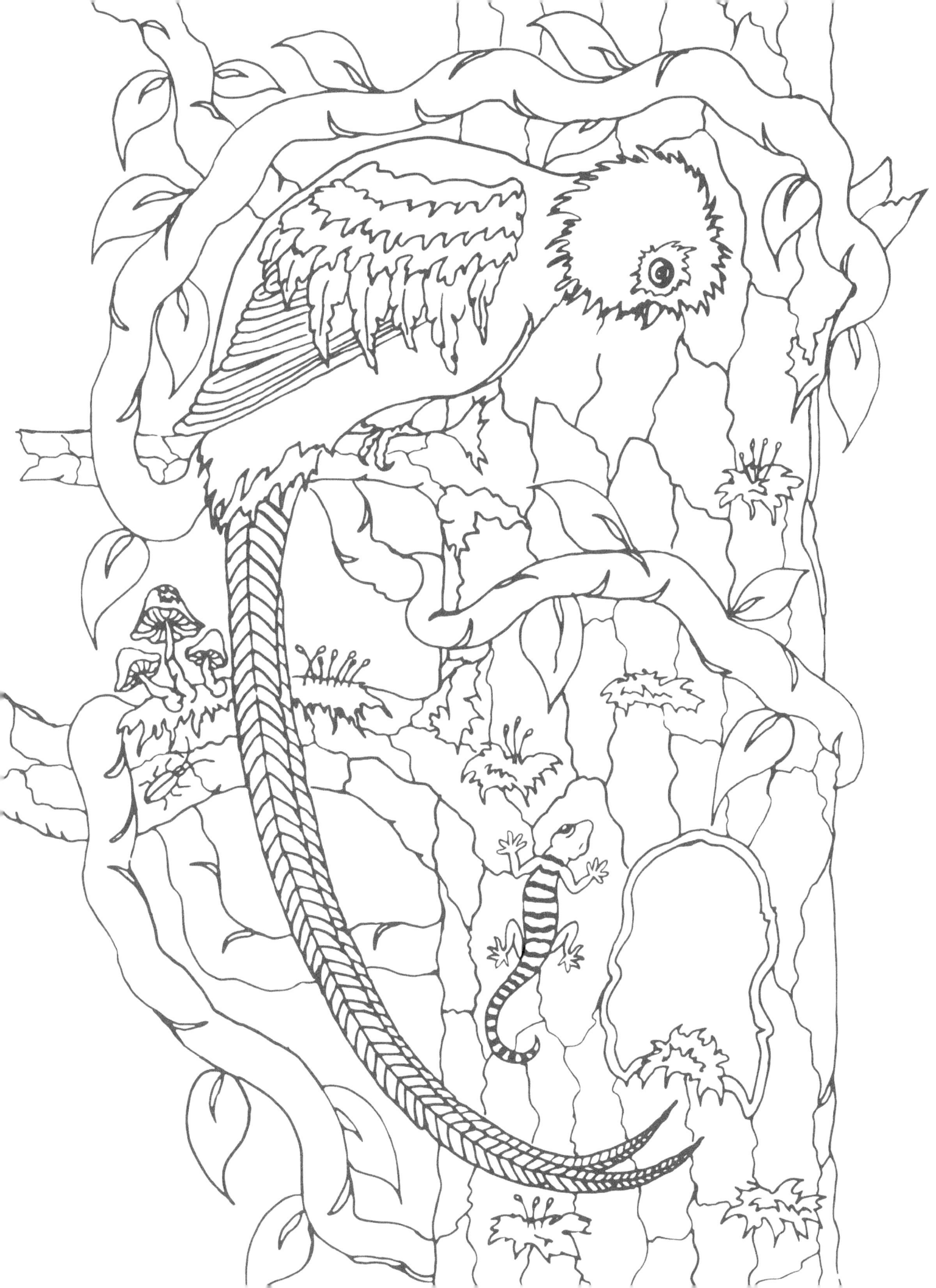

←

Resplendent quetzal
(Pharomachrus mocinno)

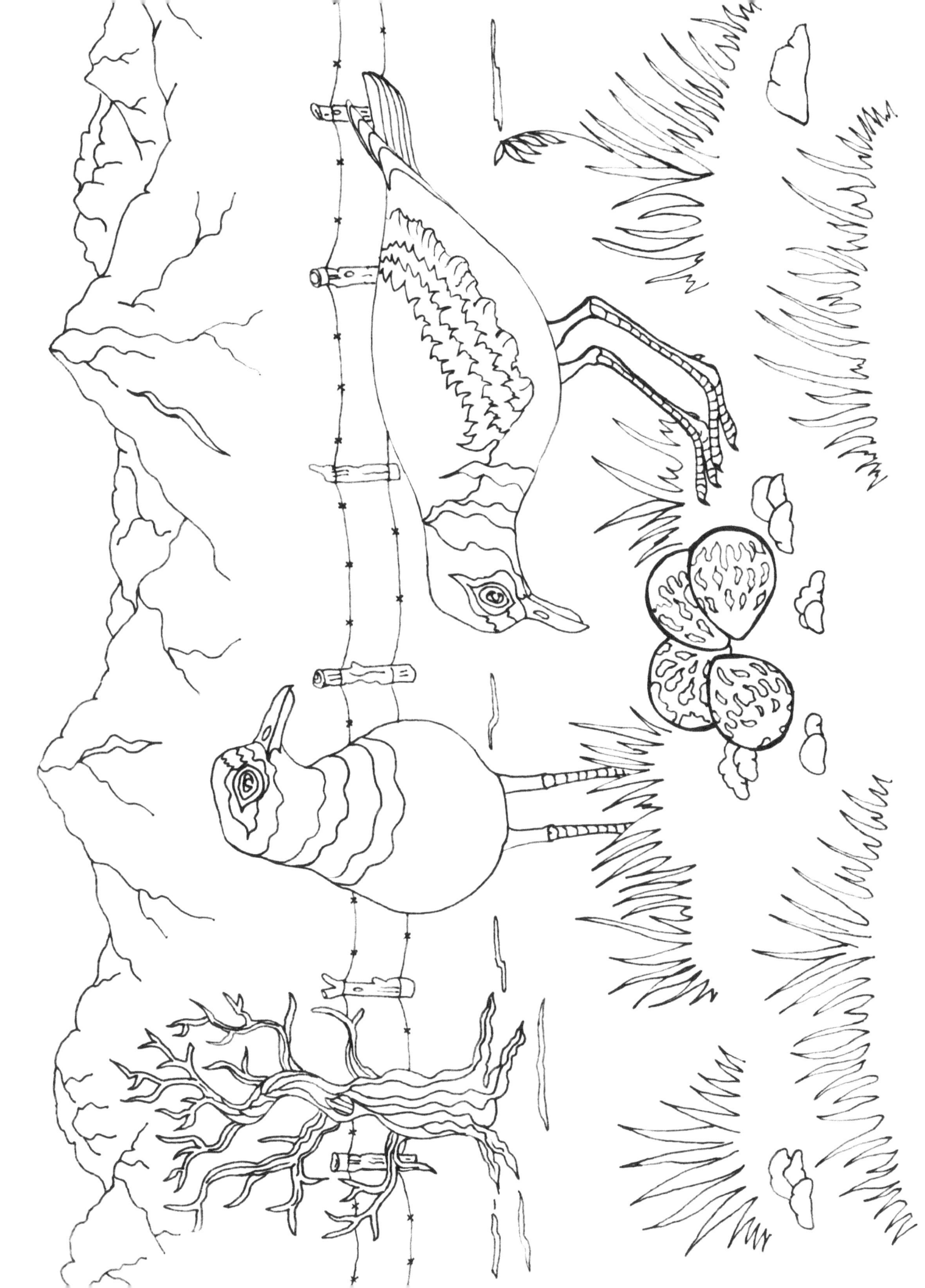

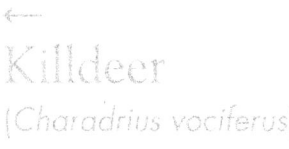

Killdeer
(*Charadrius vociferus*)

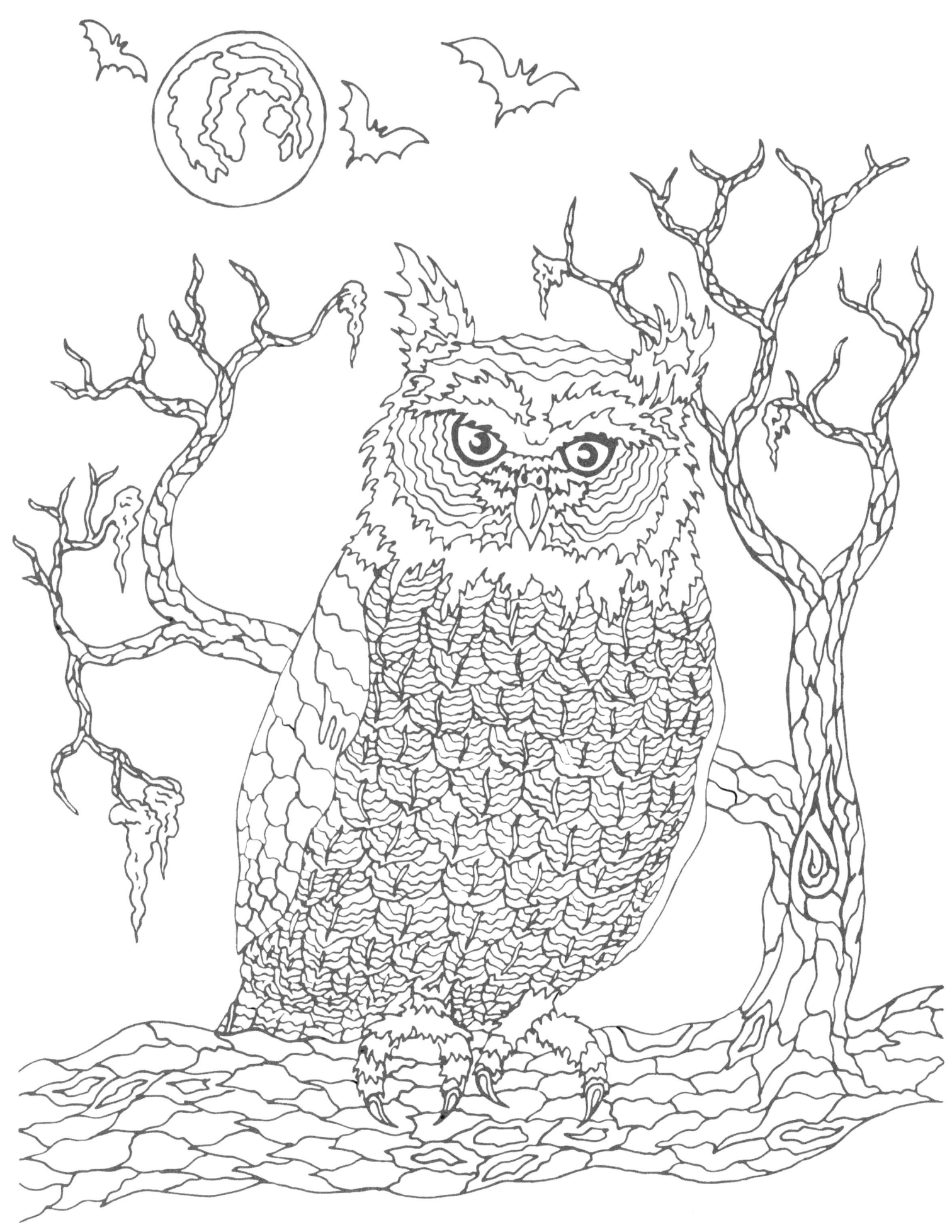

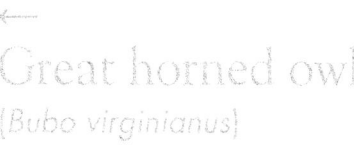

Great horned owl
(Bubo virginianus)

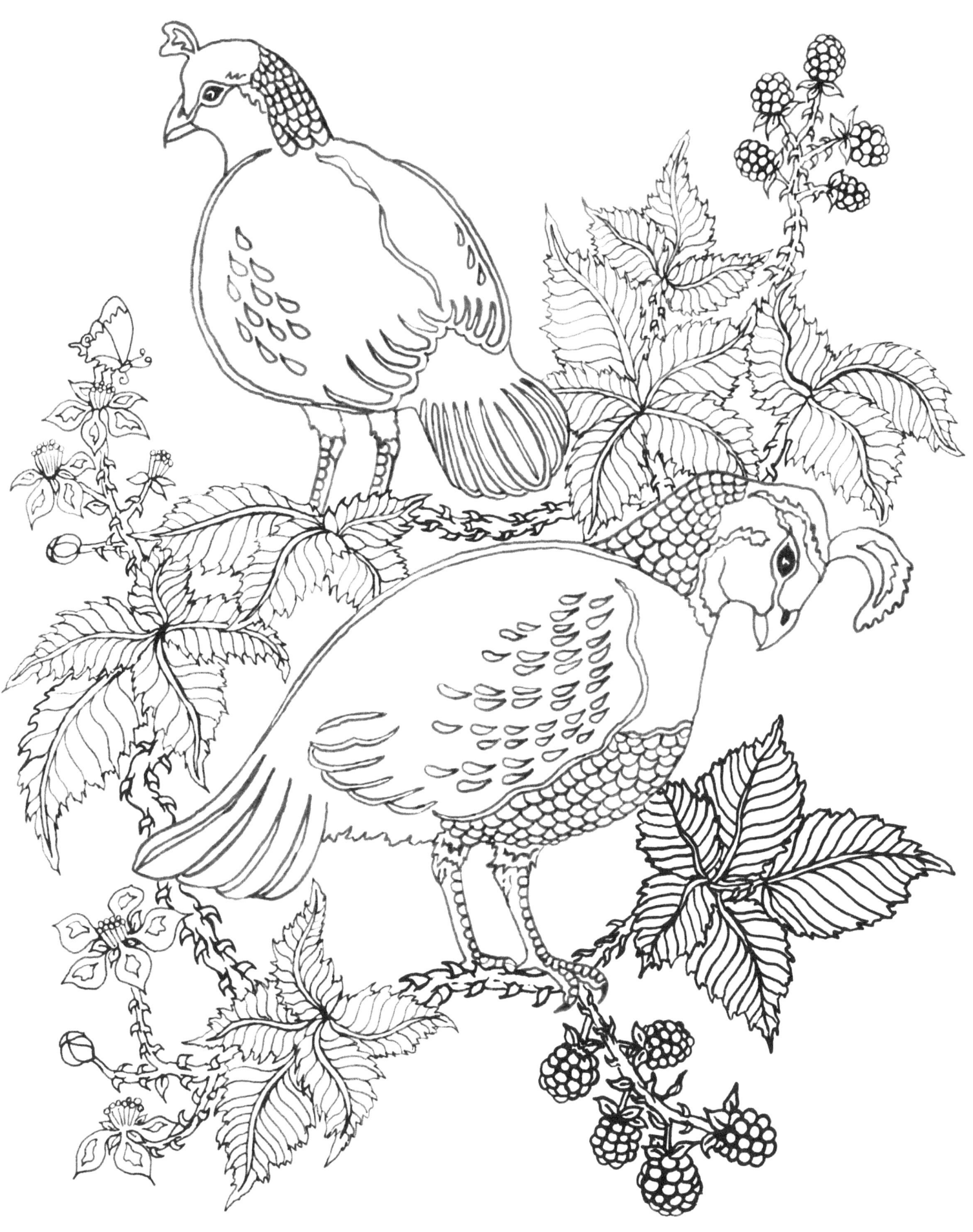

California quail

(Callipepla californica)

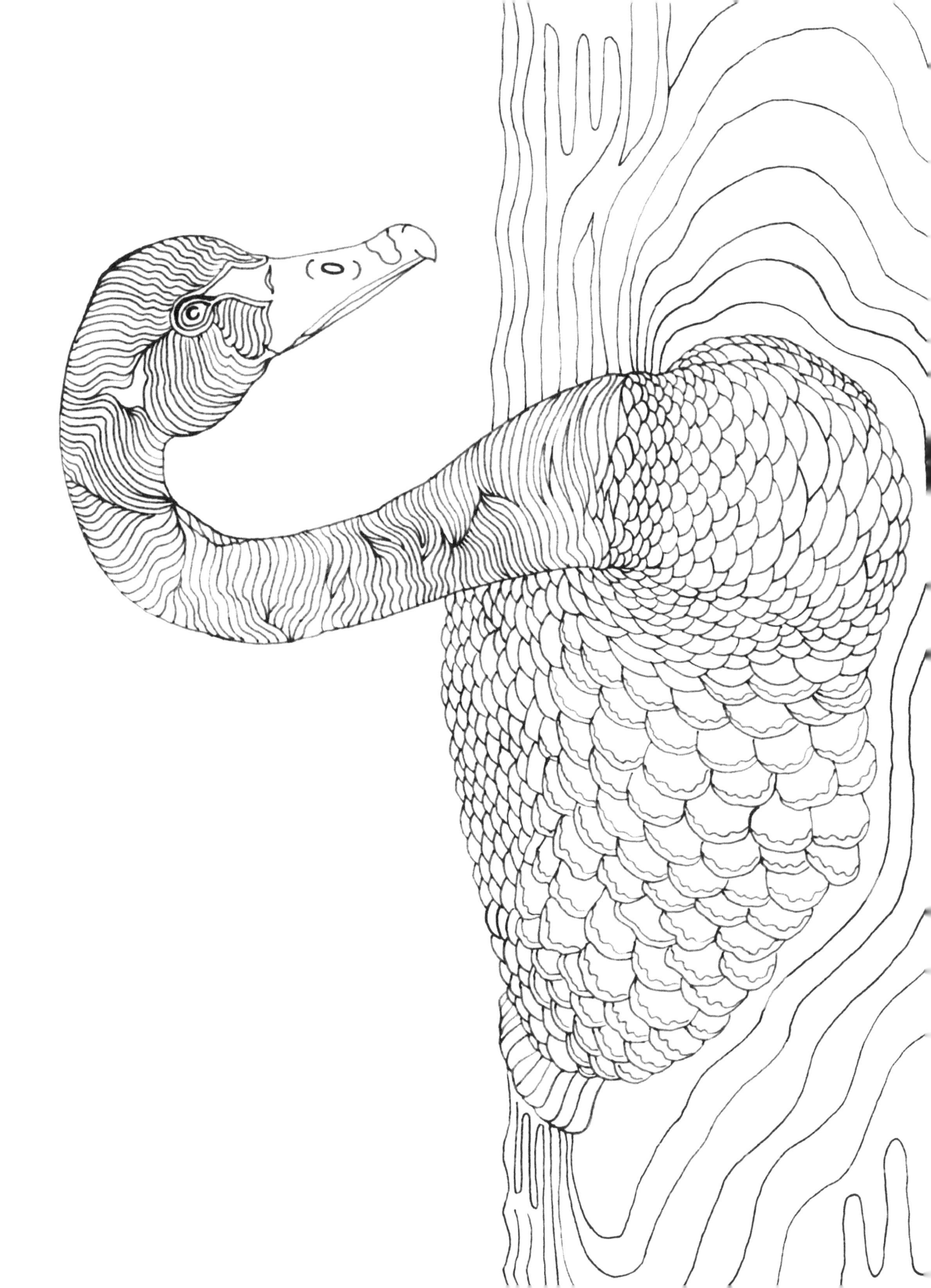

←

Black swan
(Cygnus atratus)

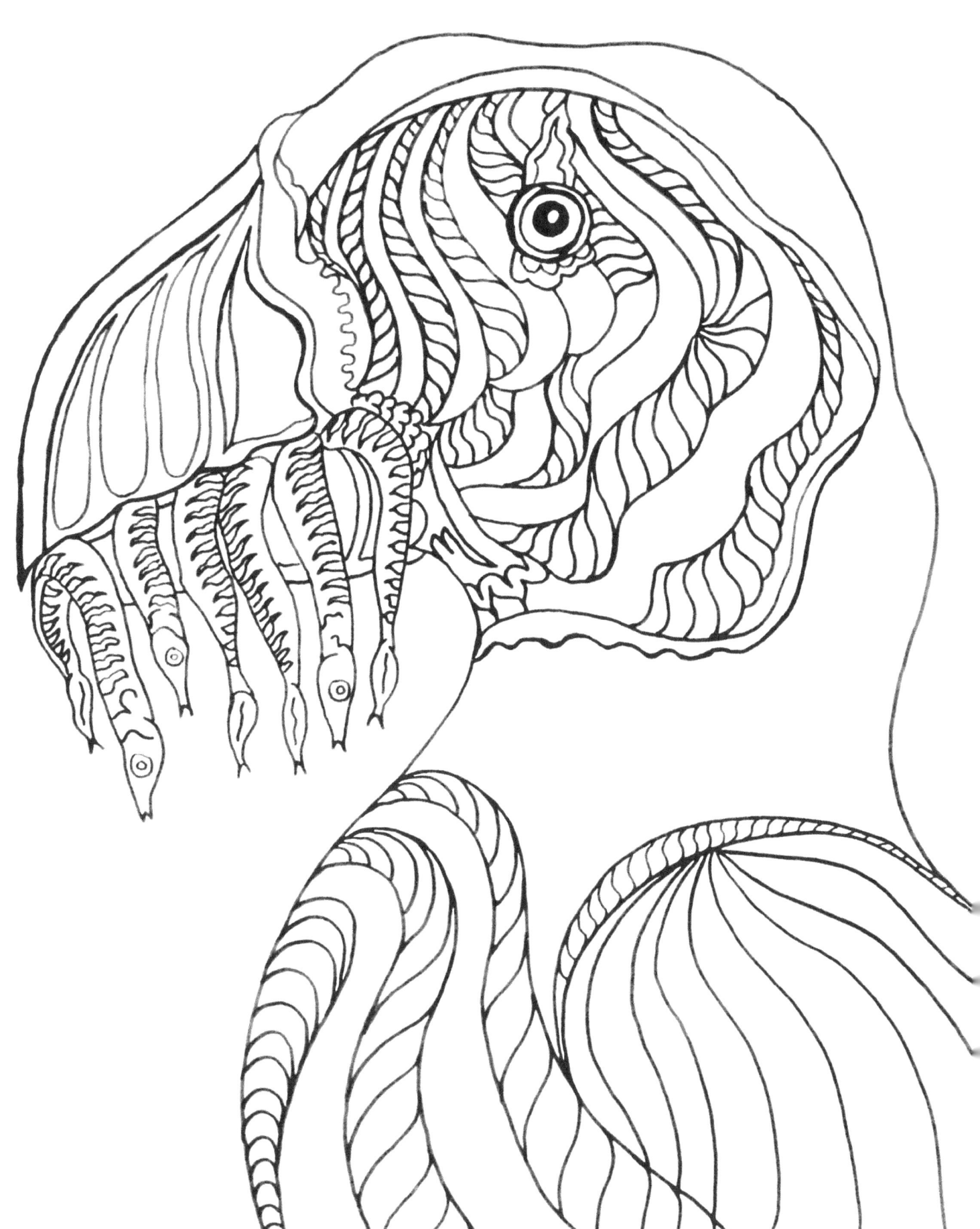

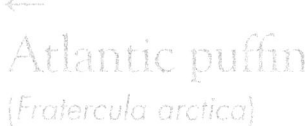

Atlantic puffin
(Fratercula arctica)

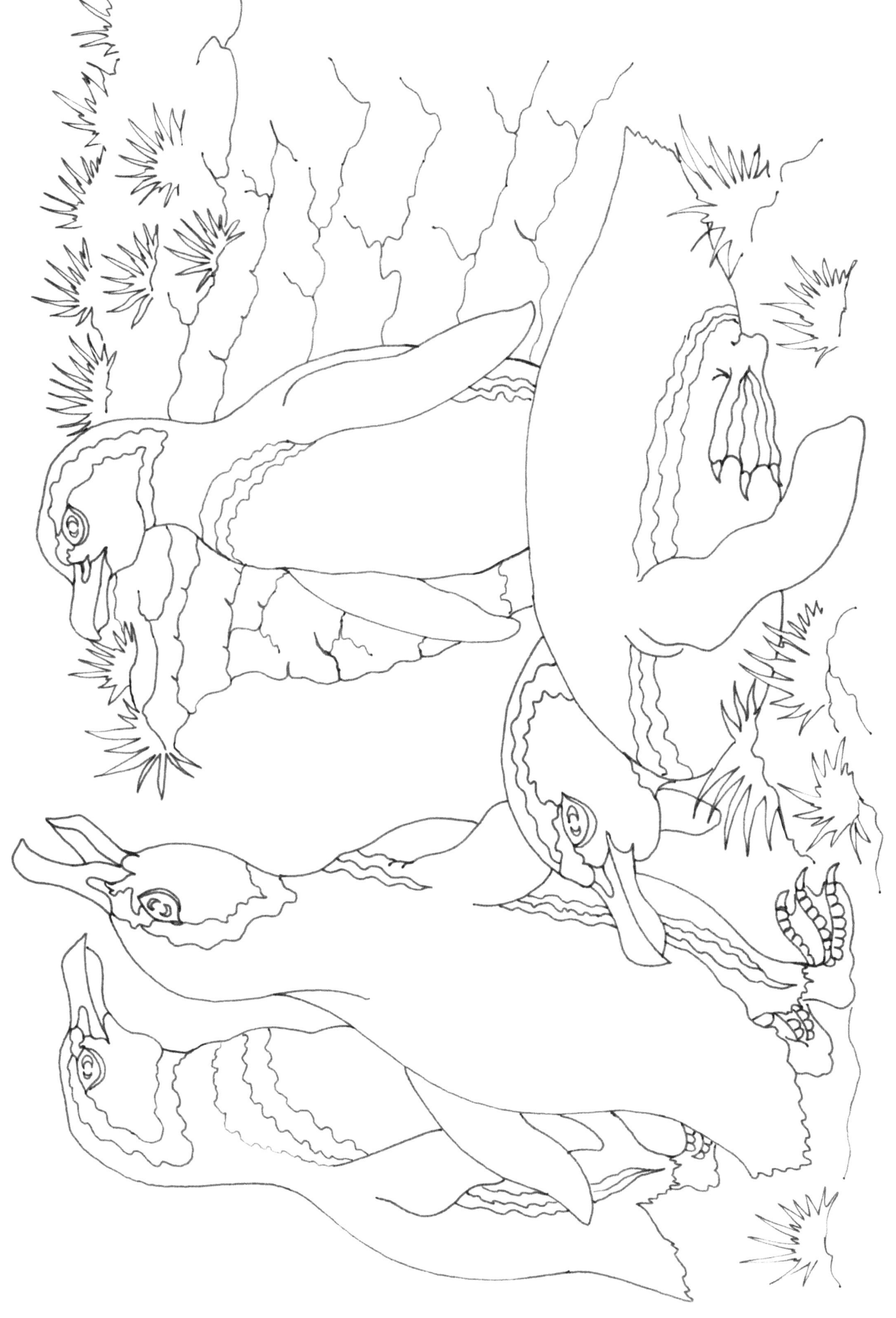

Magellanic penguins
(Spheniscus magellanicus)

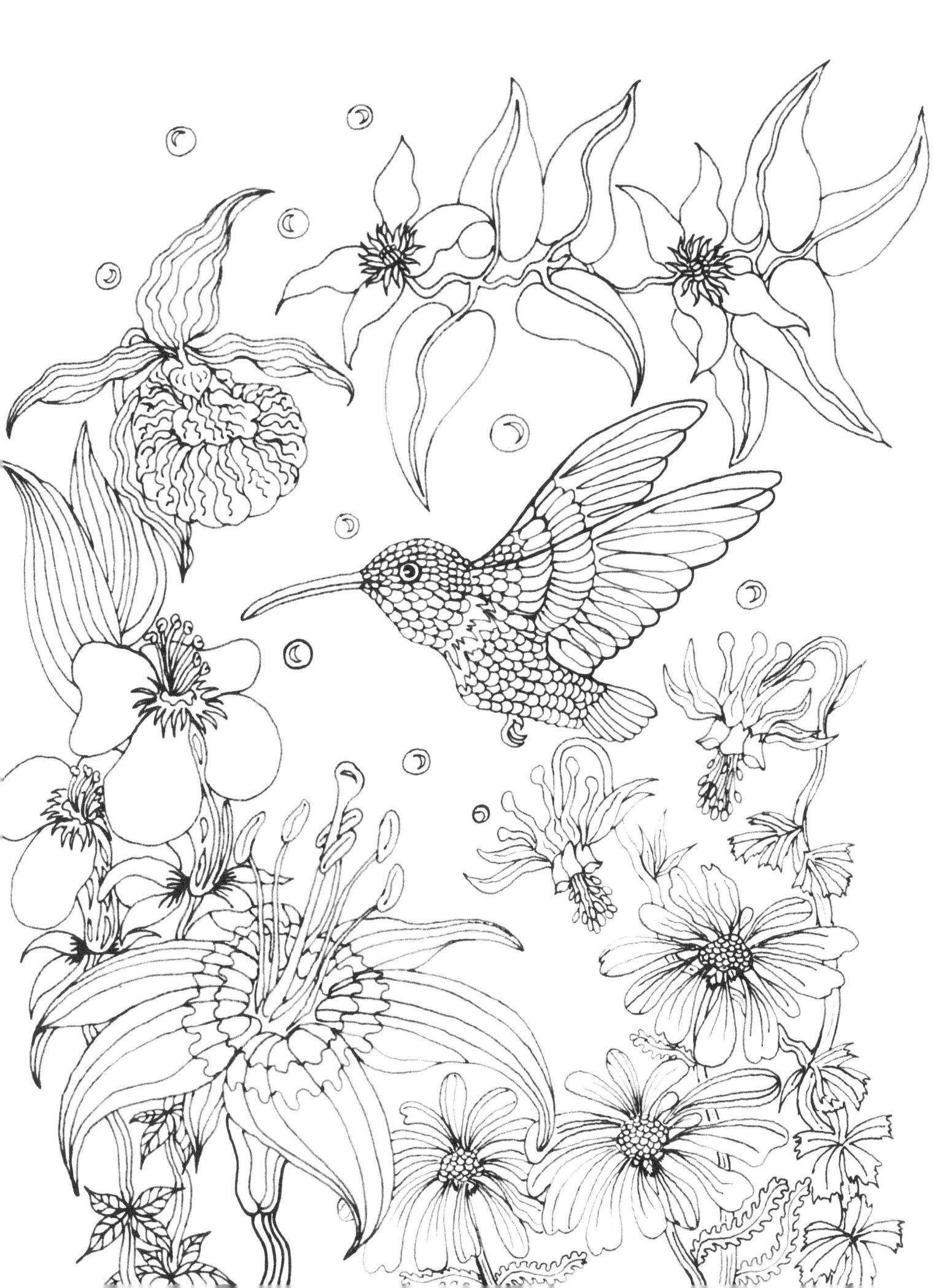

Rufous hummingbird
(*Selasphorus rufus*)

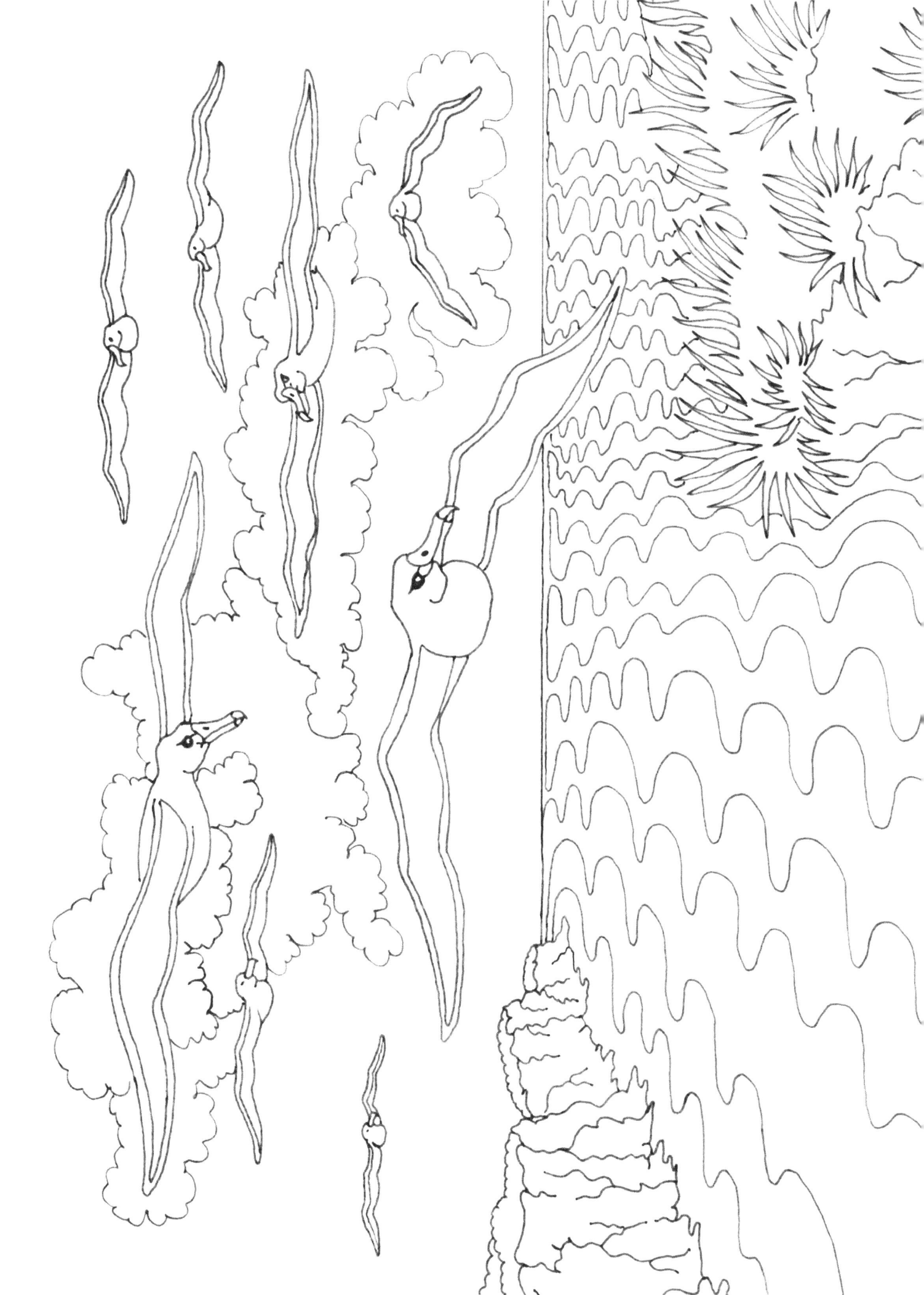

←

Laysan albatross
(*Phoebastria immutabilis*)

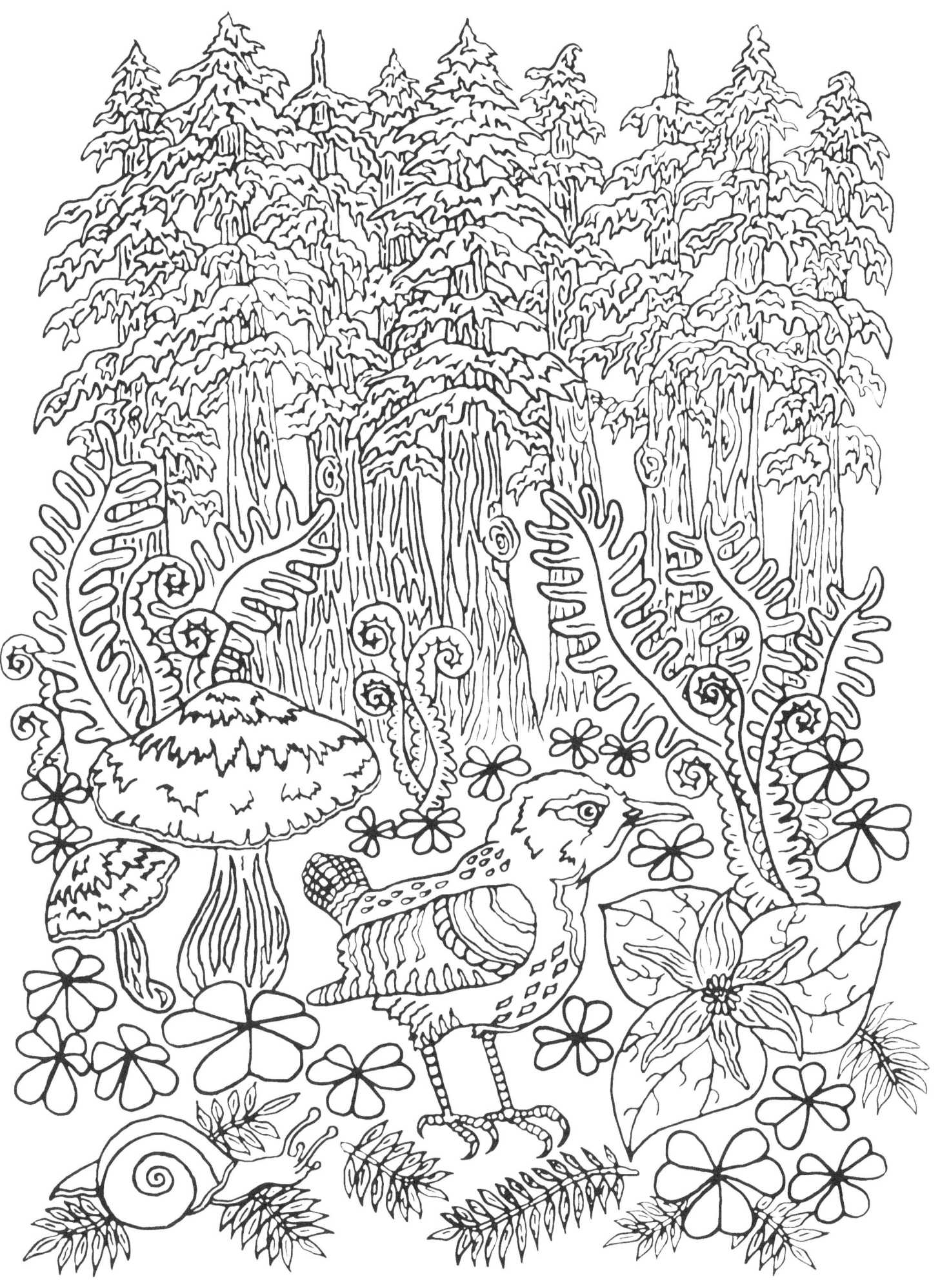

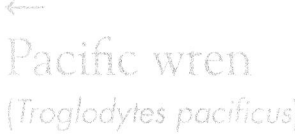

Pacific wren
(*Troglodytes pacificus*)

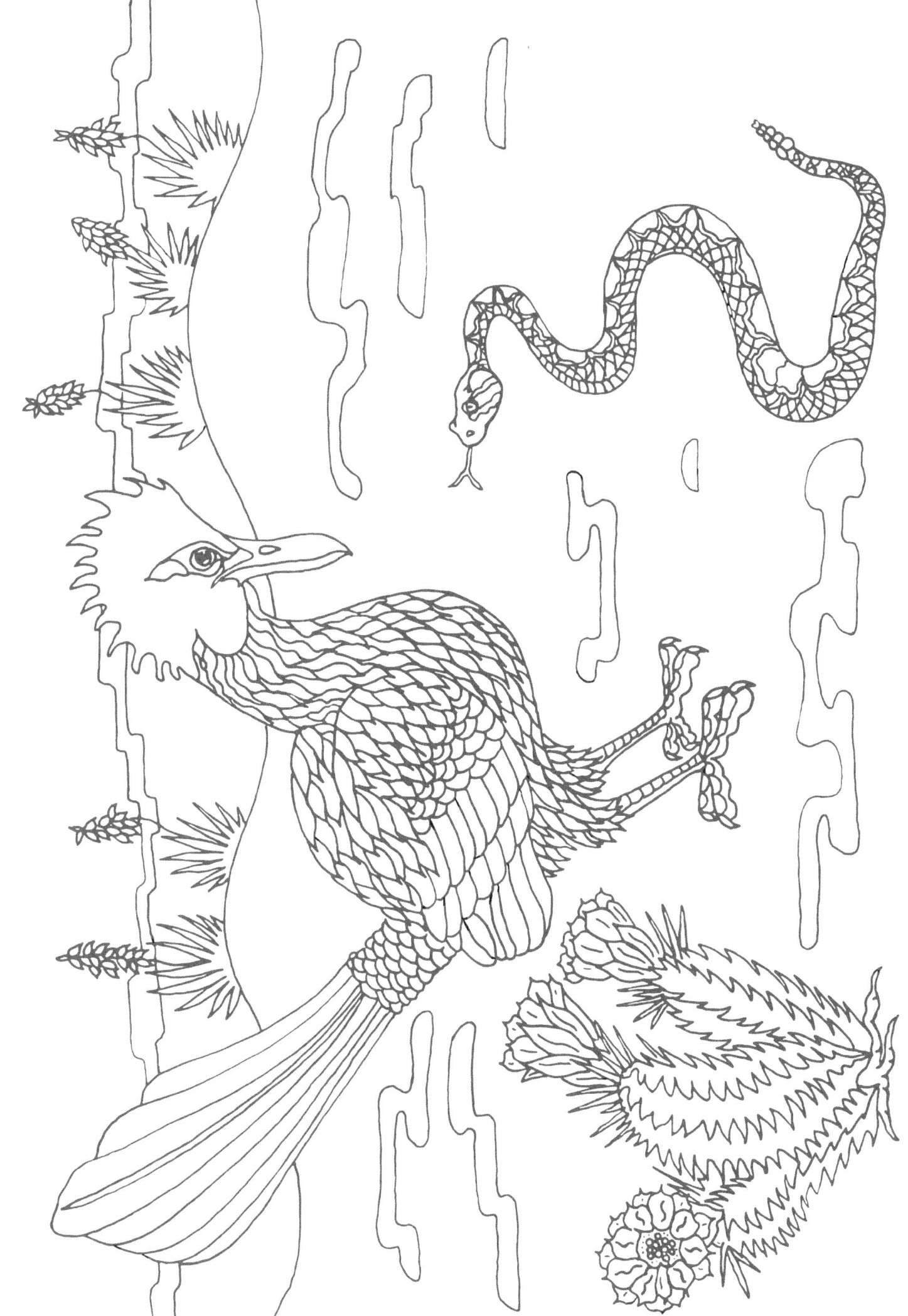

← Greater roadrunner
(*Geococcyx californianus*)

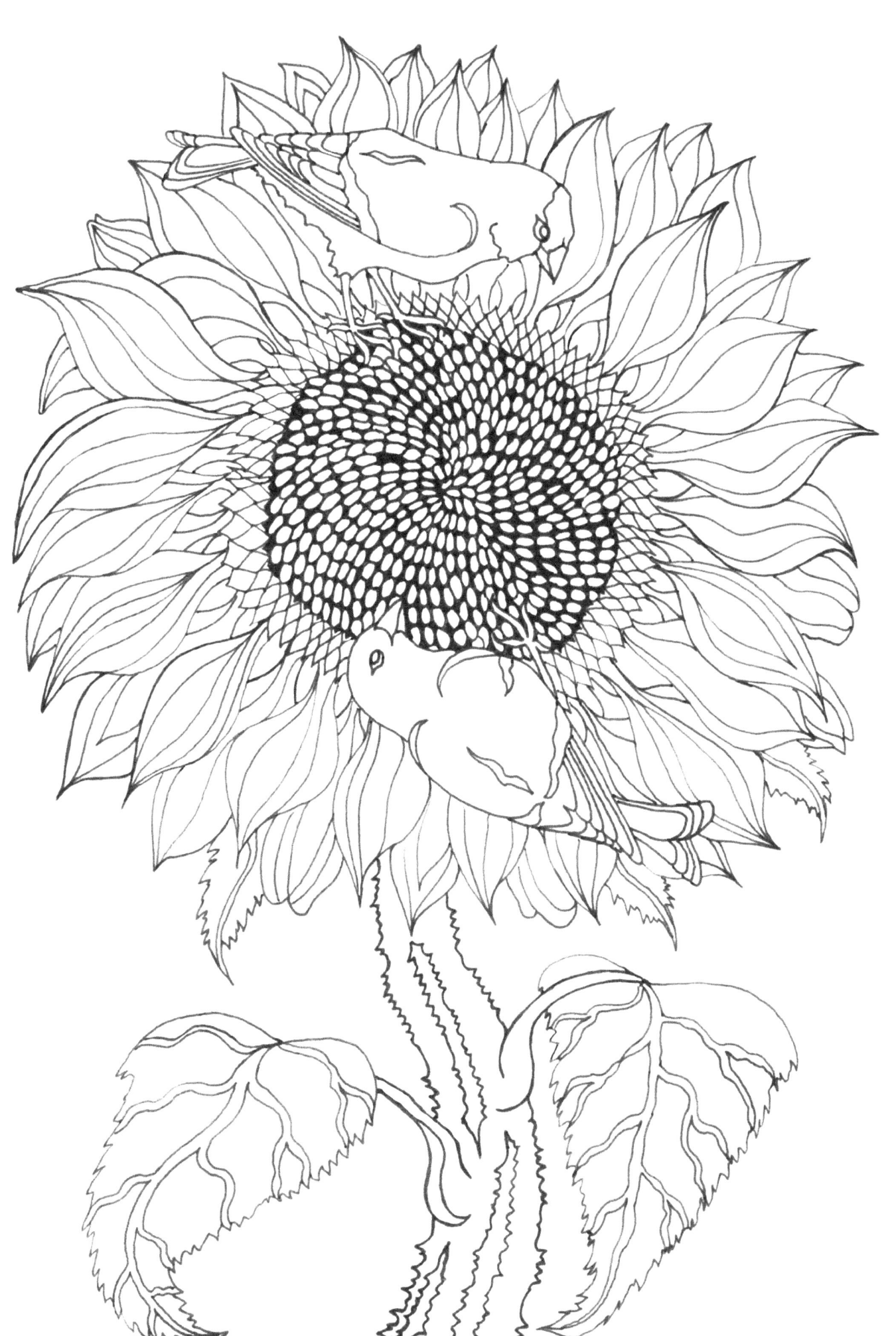

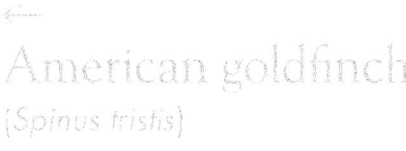

American goldfinch
(*Spinus tristis*)

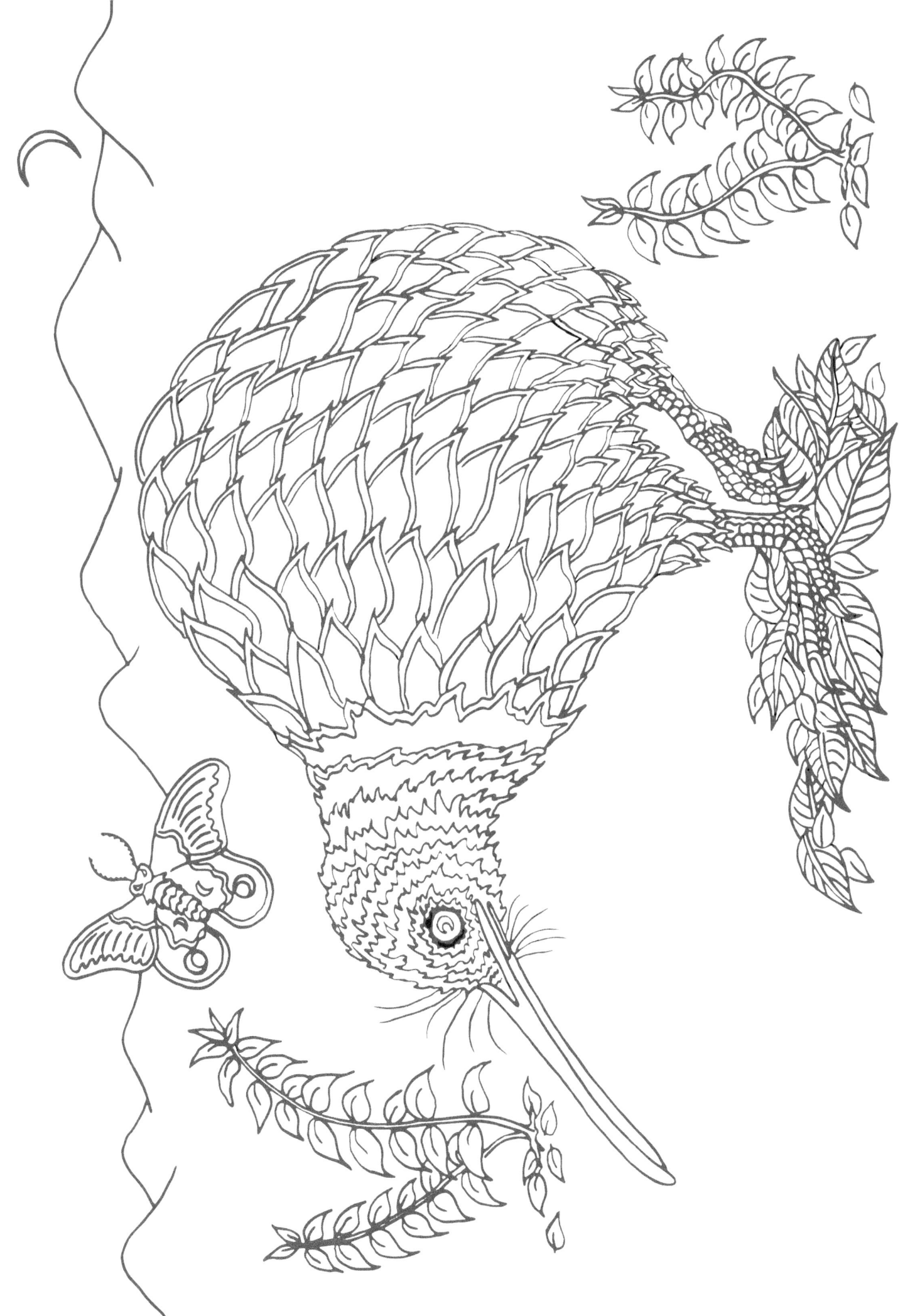

←

Brown kiwi
(*Apteryx mantelli*)

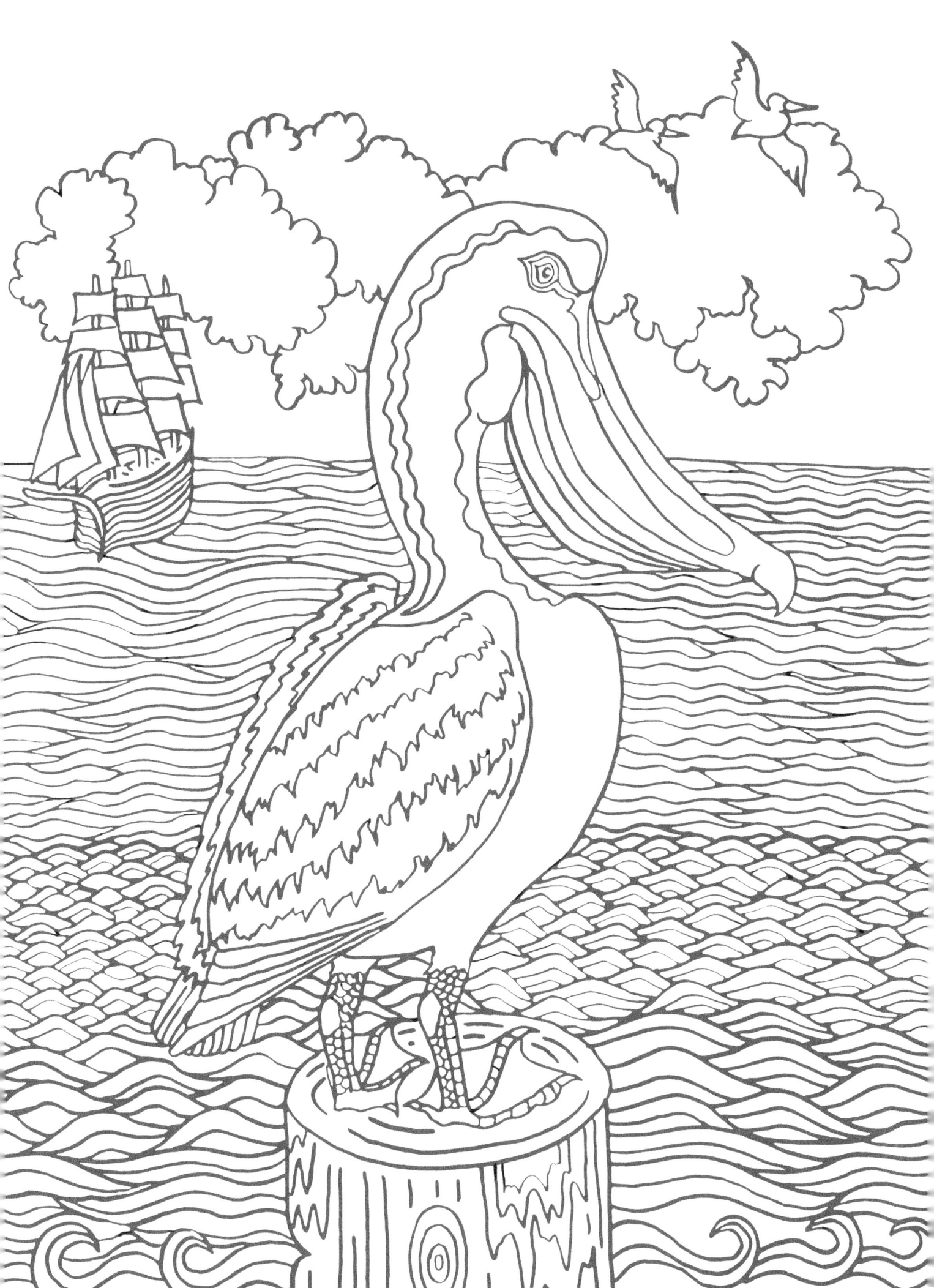

←

Brown pelican
(Pelecanus occidentalis)

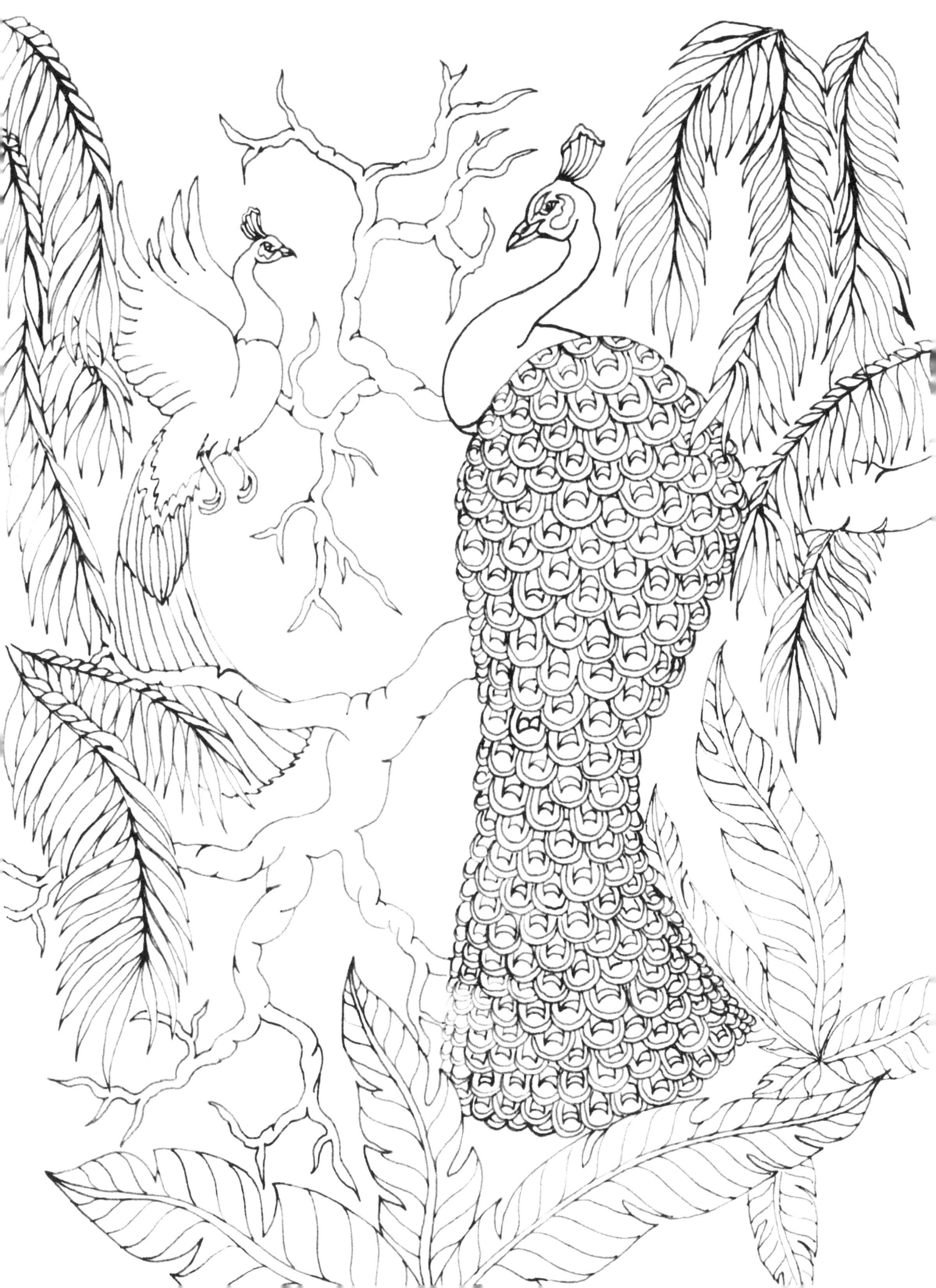

←

Indian peafowl
(Pavo cristatus)

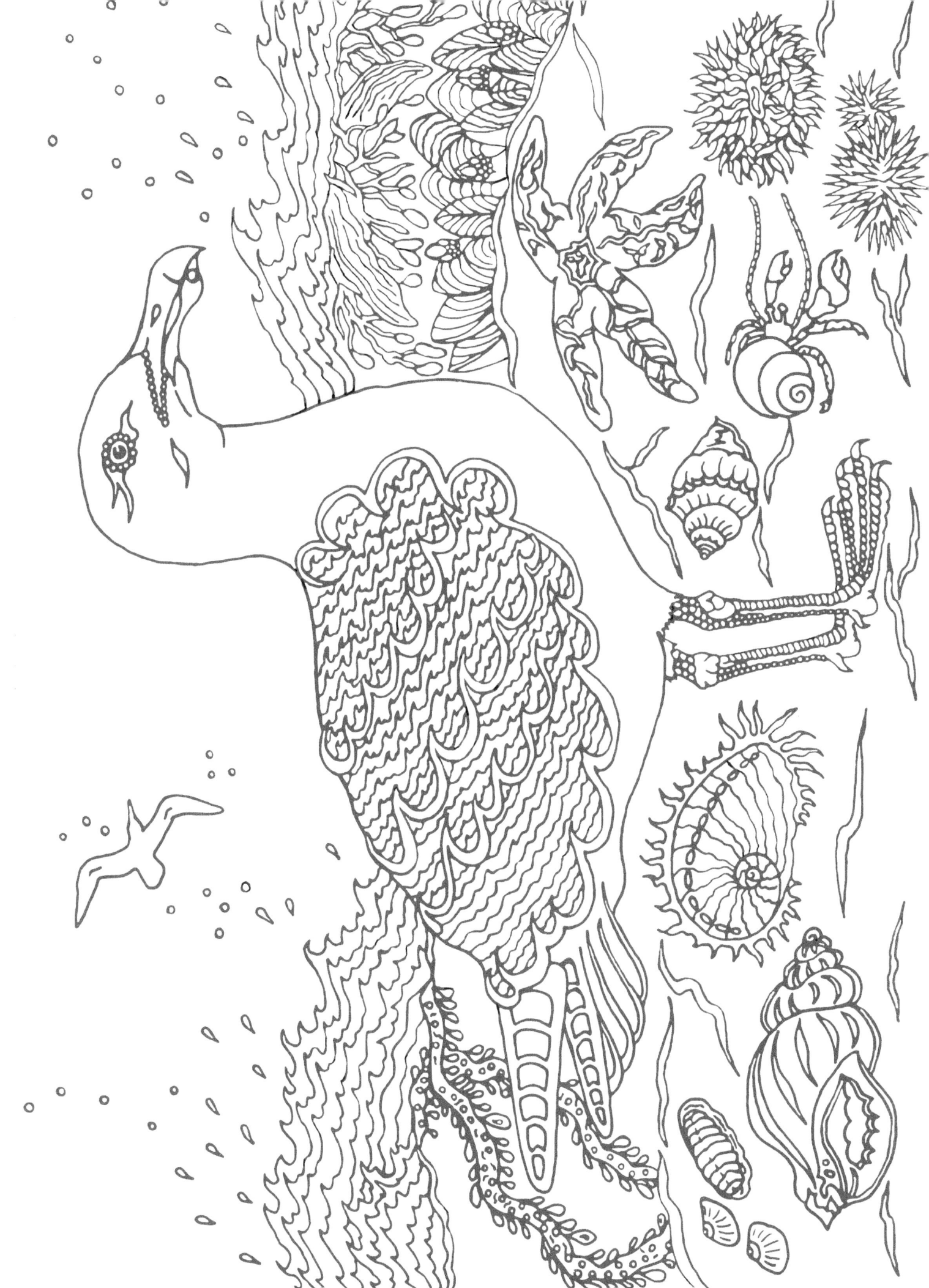

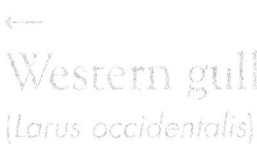

Western gull

(*Larus occidentalis*)

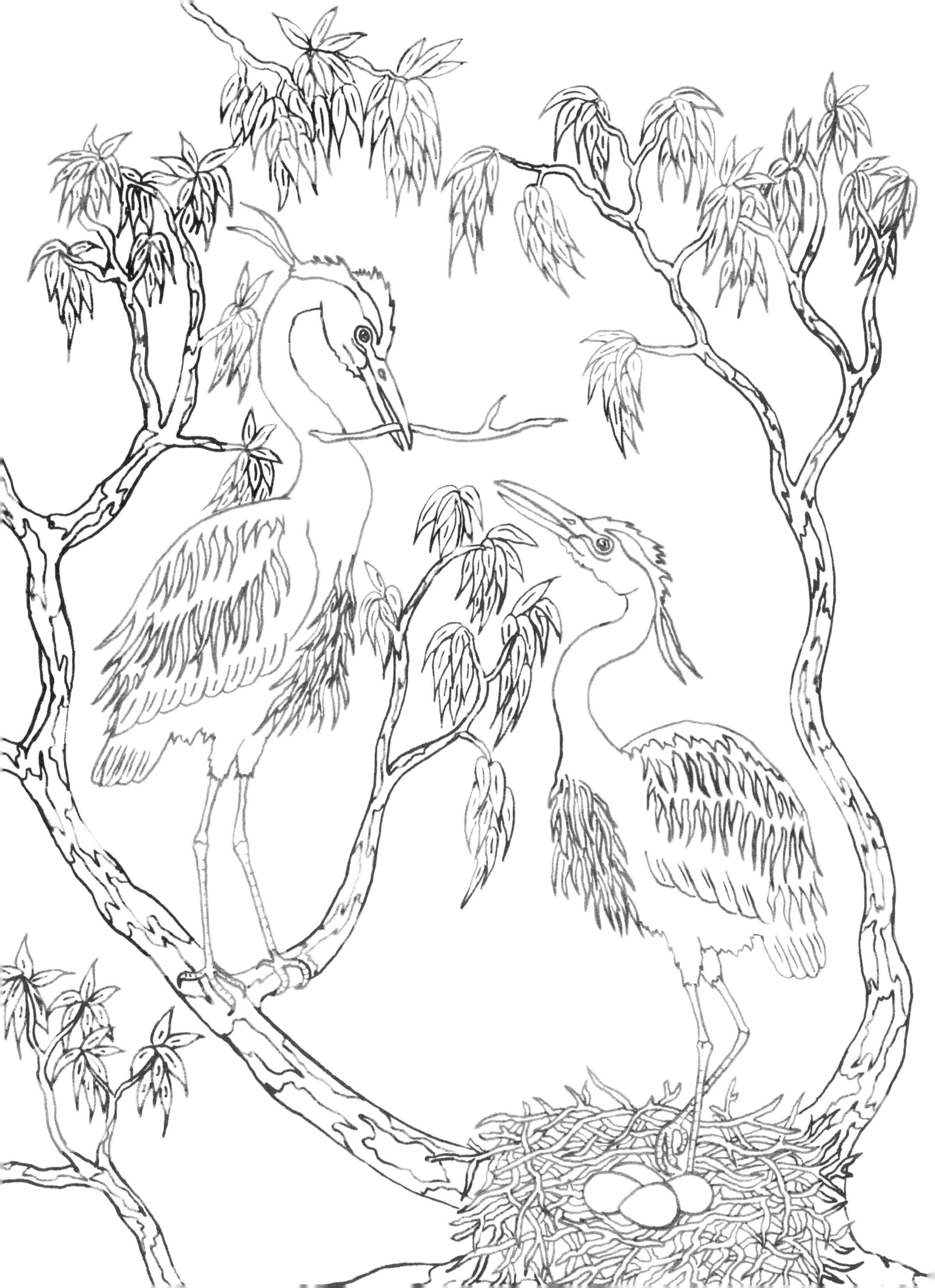

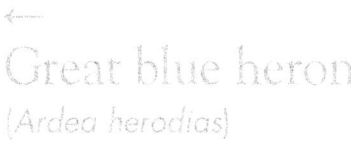

Great blue heron
(*Ardea herodias*)

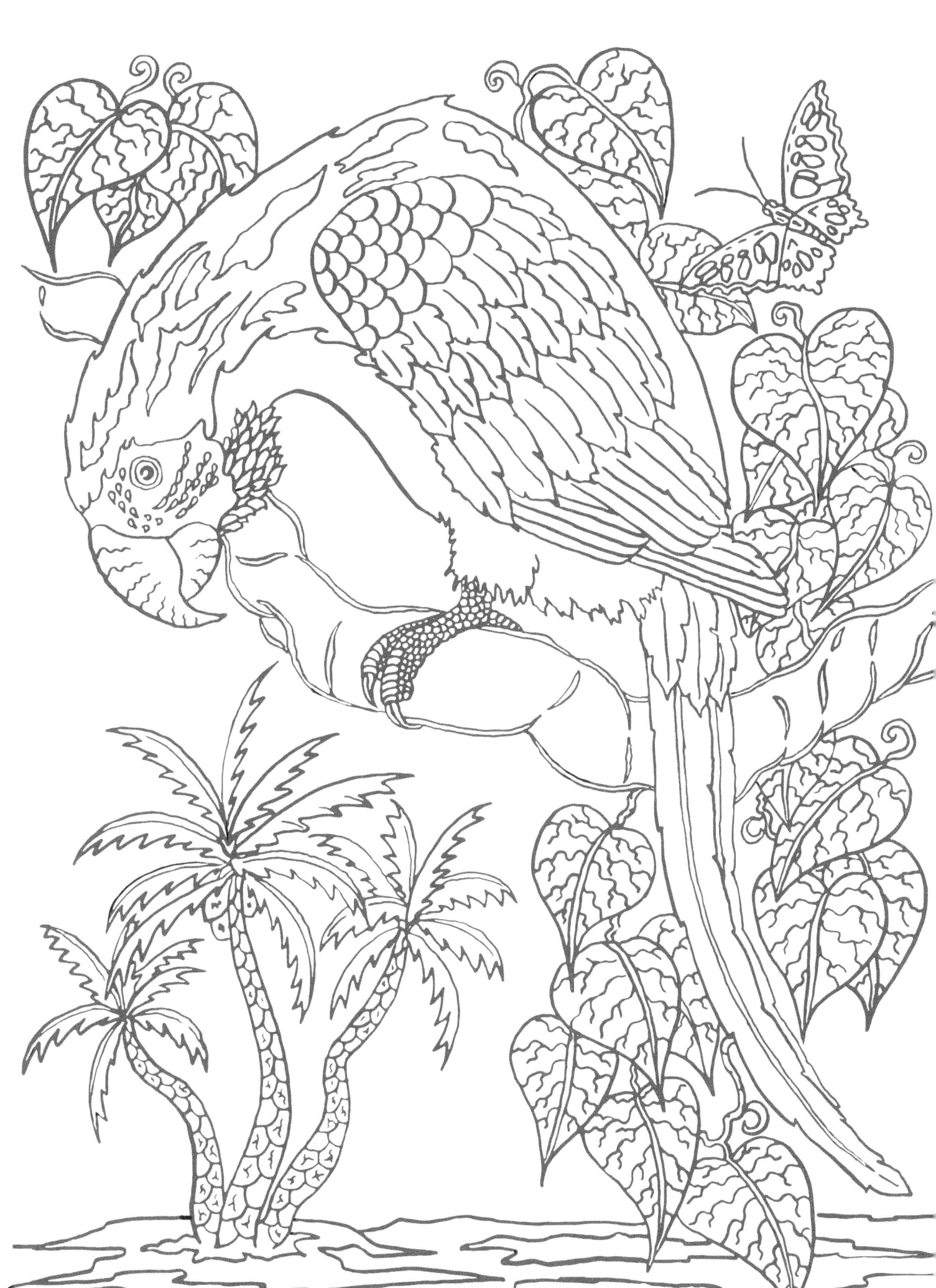

Blue and gold macaw
(*Ara ararauna*)

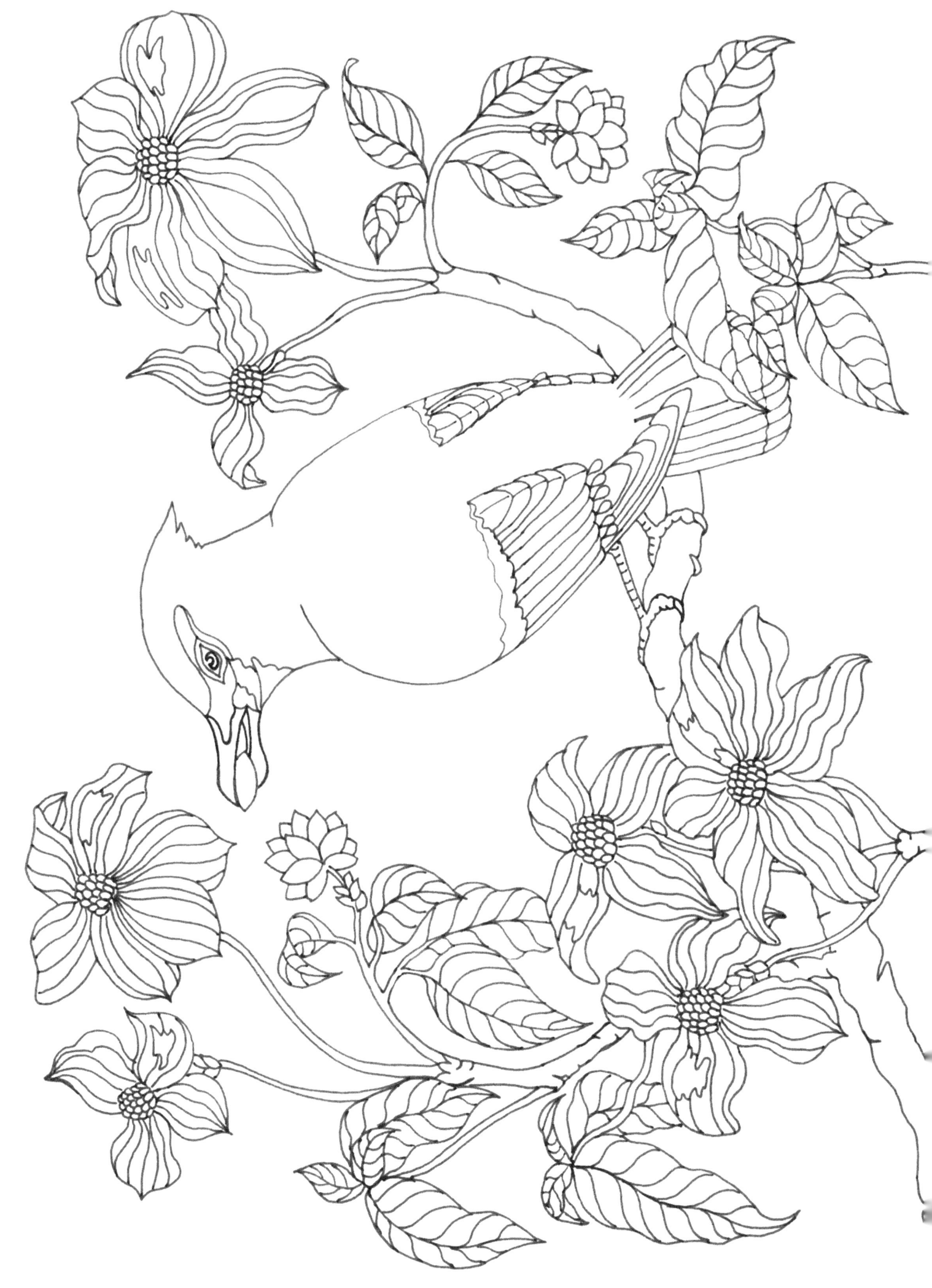

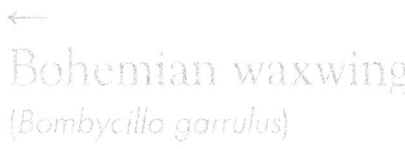

Bohemian waxwing
(Bombycilla garrulus)

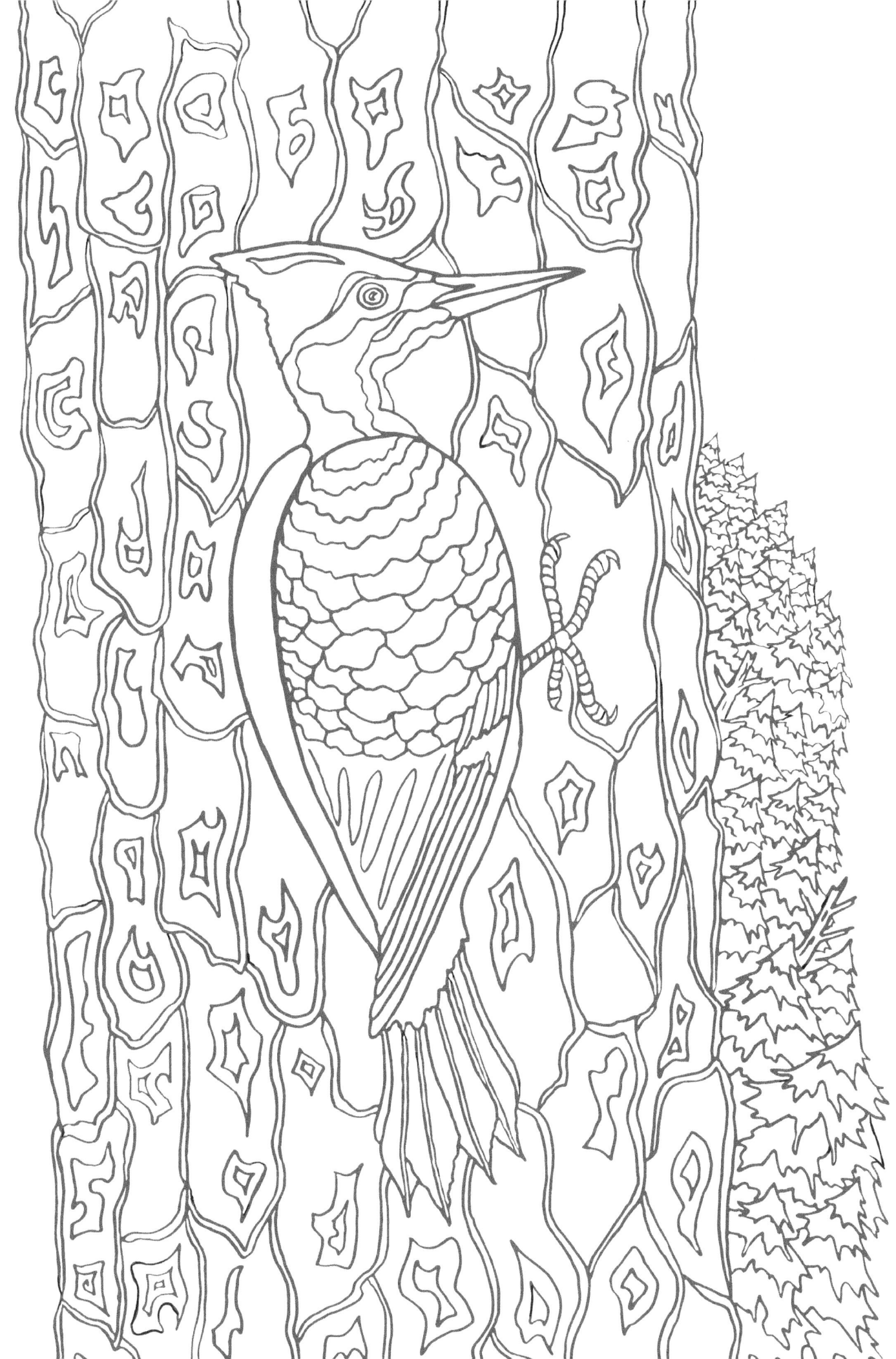

← ⋯

Pileated woodpecker
(*Dryocopus pileatus*)

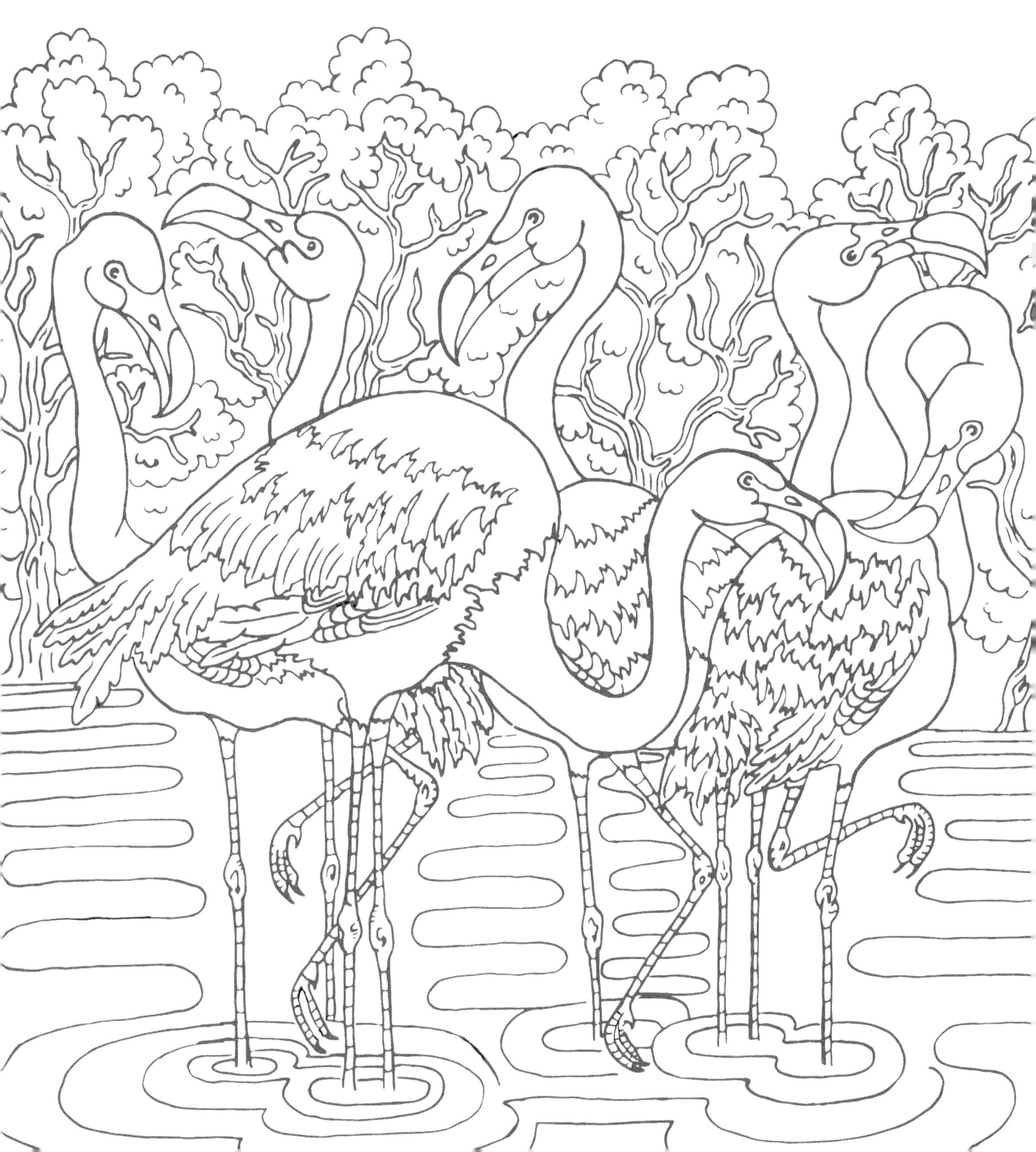

←

Greater flamingo
(*Phoenicopterus roseus*)

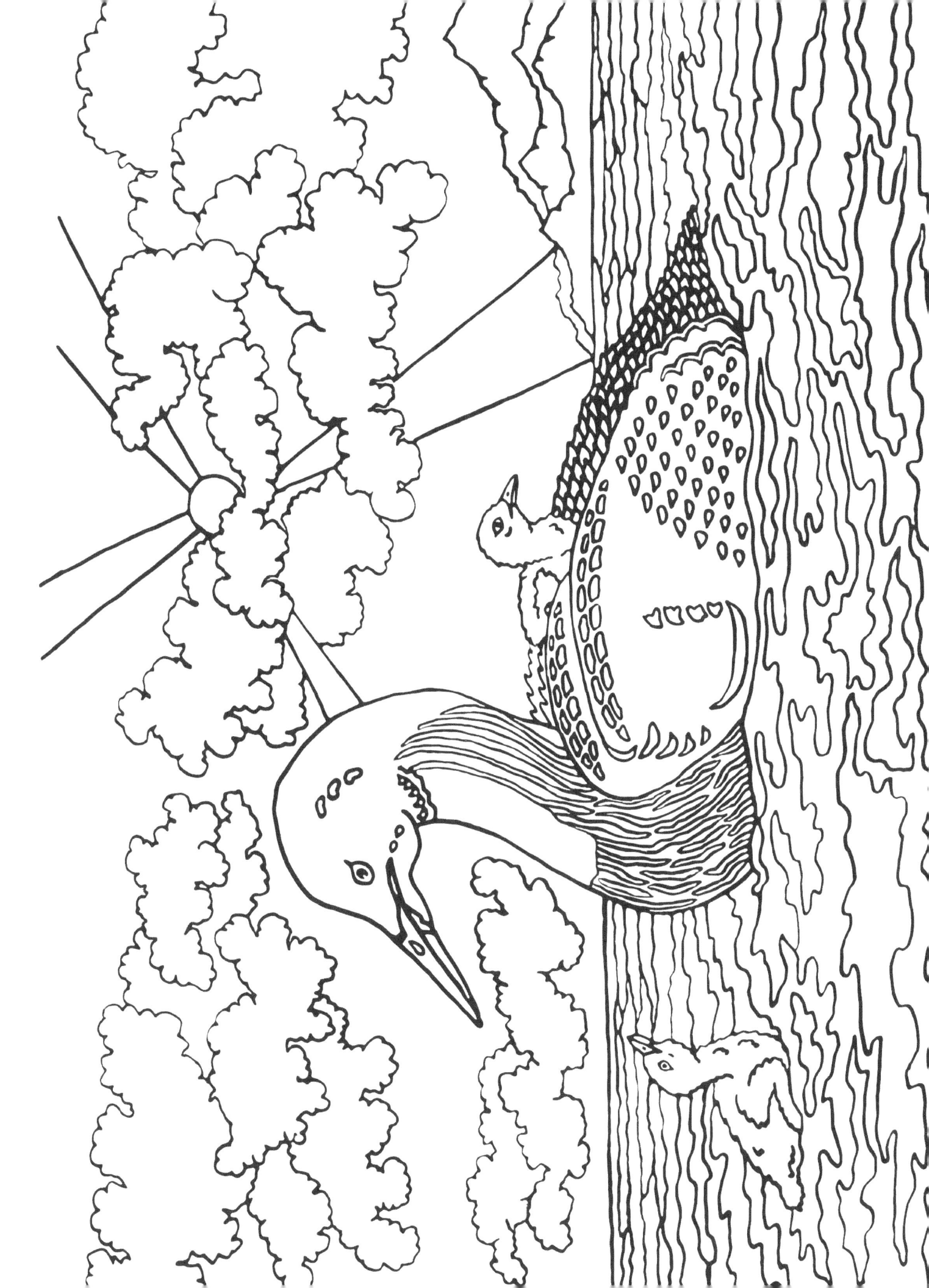

← ——

Pacific loon
(*Gavia pacifica*)

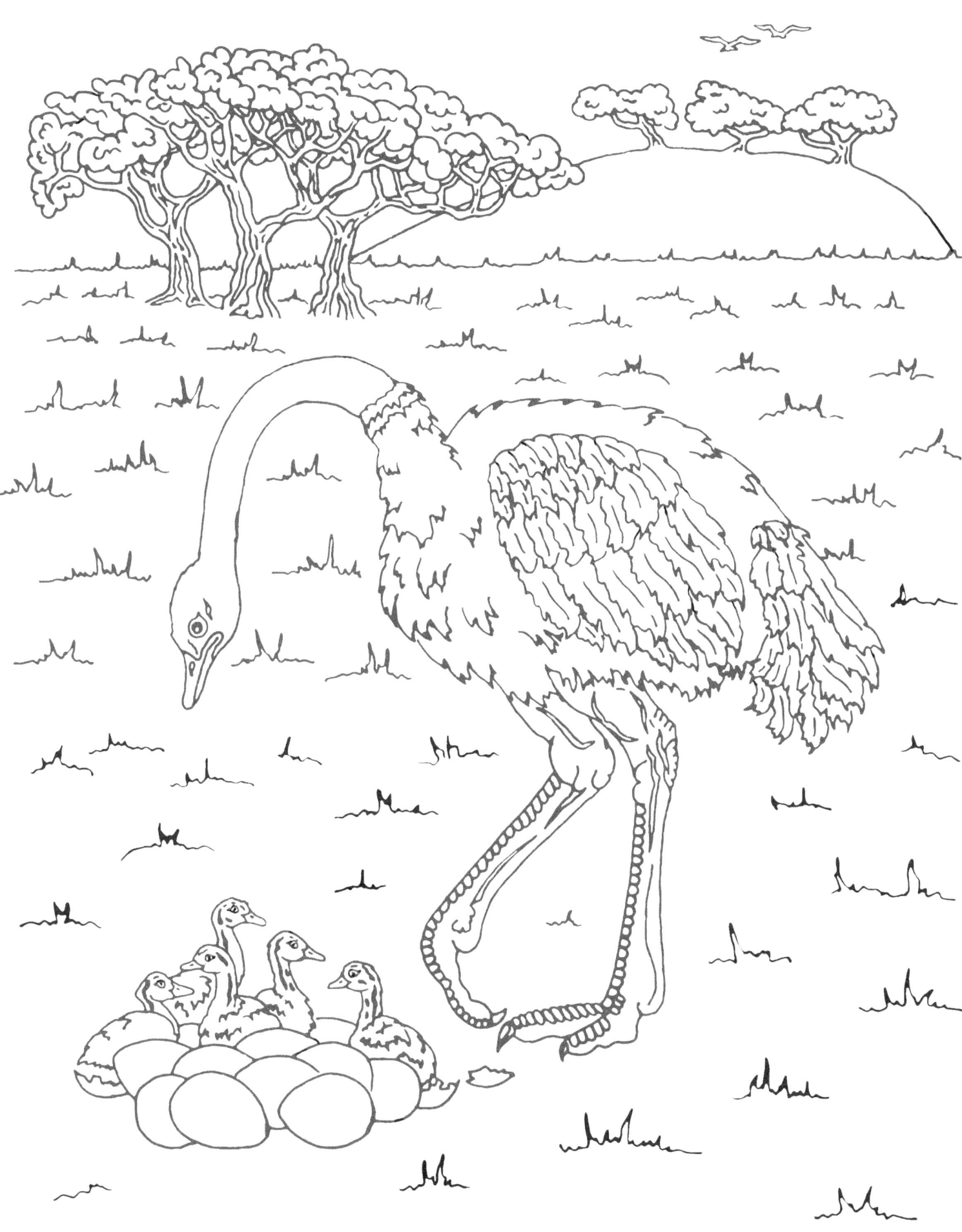

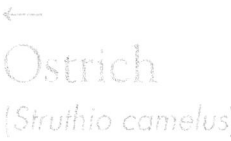

Ostrich
(Struthio camelus)

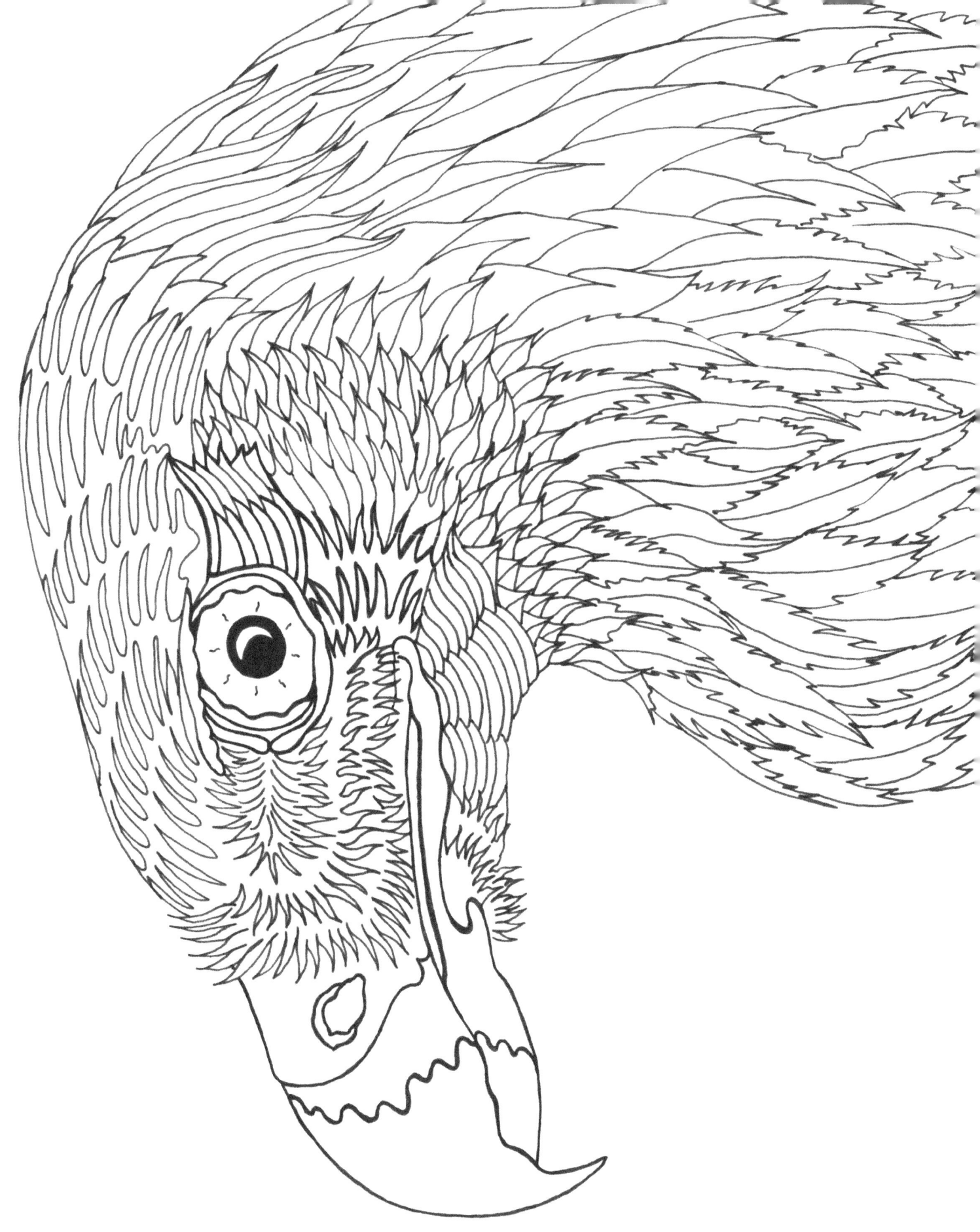

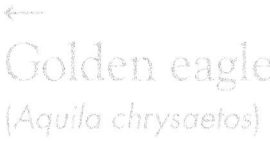

Golden eagle
(*Aquila chrysaetos*)

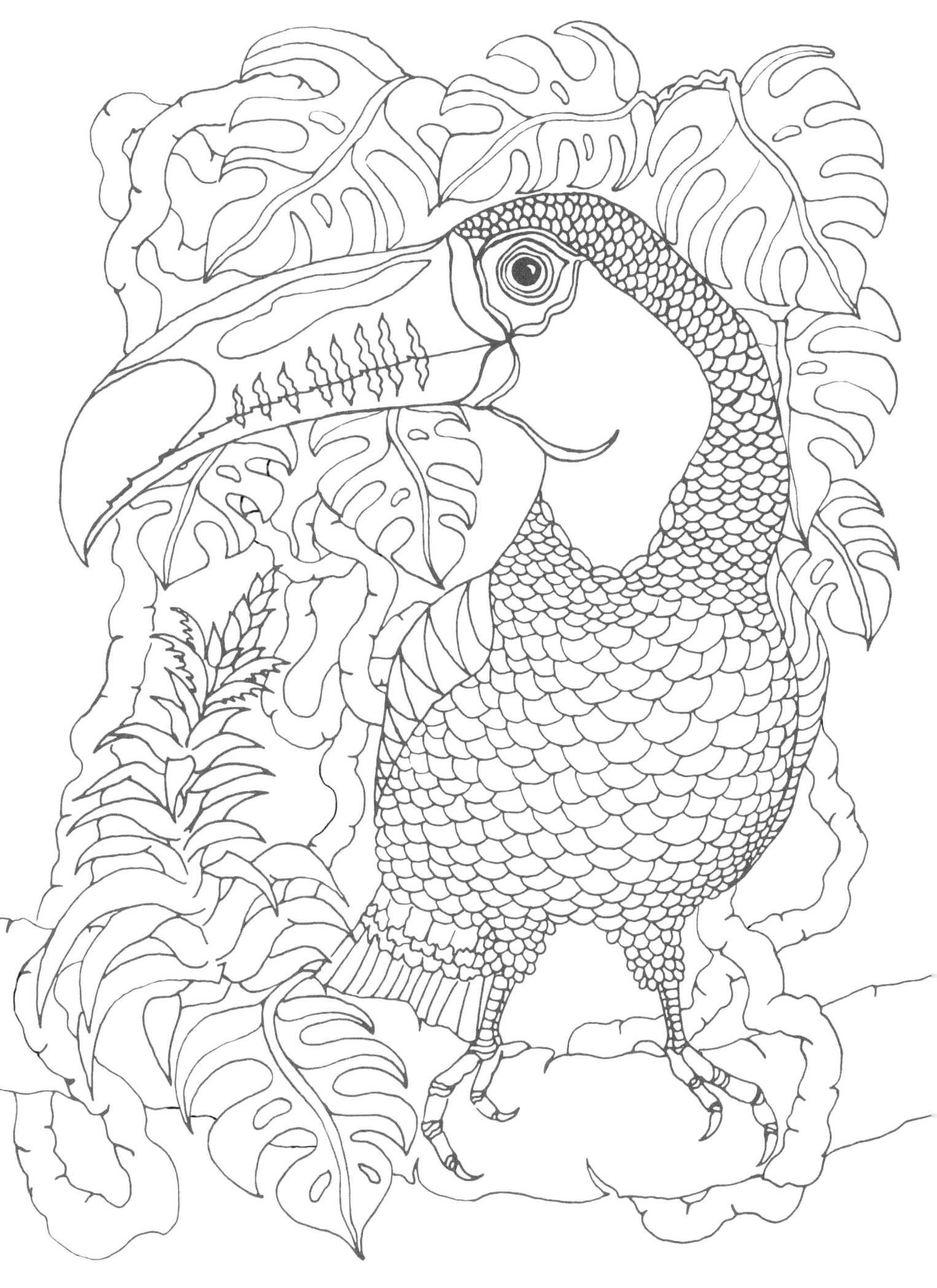

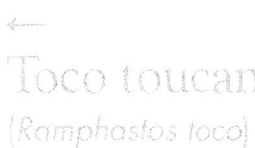

Toco toucan
(*Ramphastos toco*)

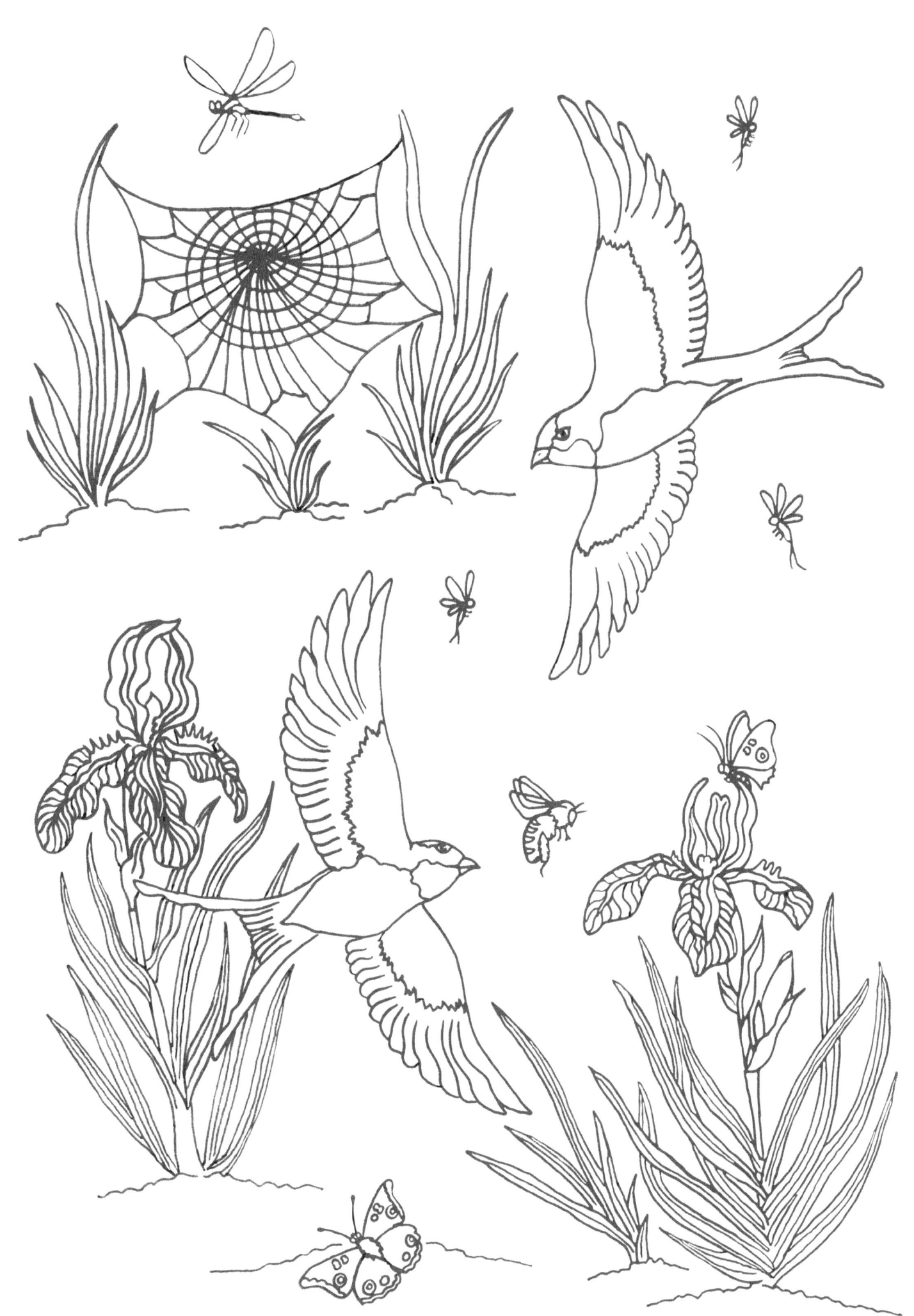

Barn swallows
(Hirundo rustica)

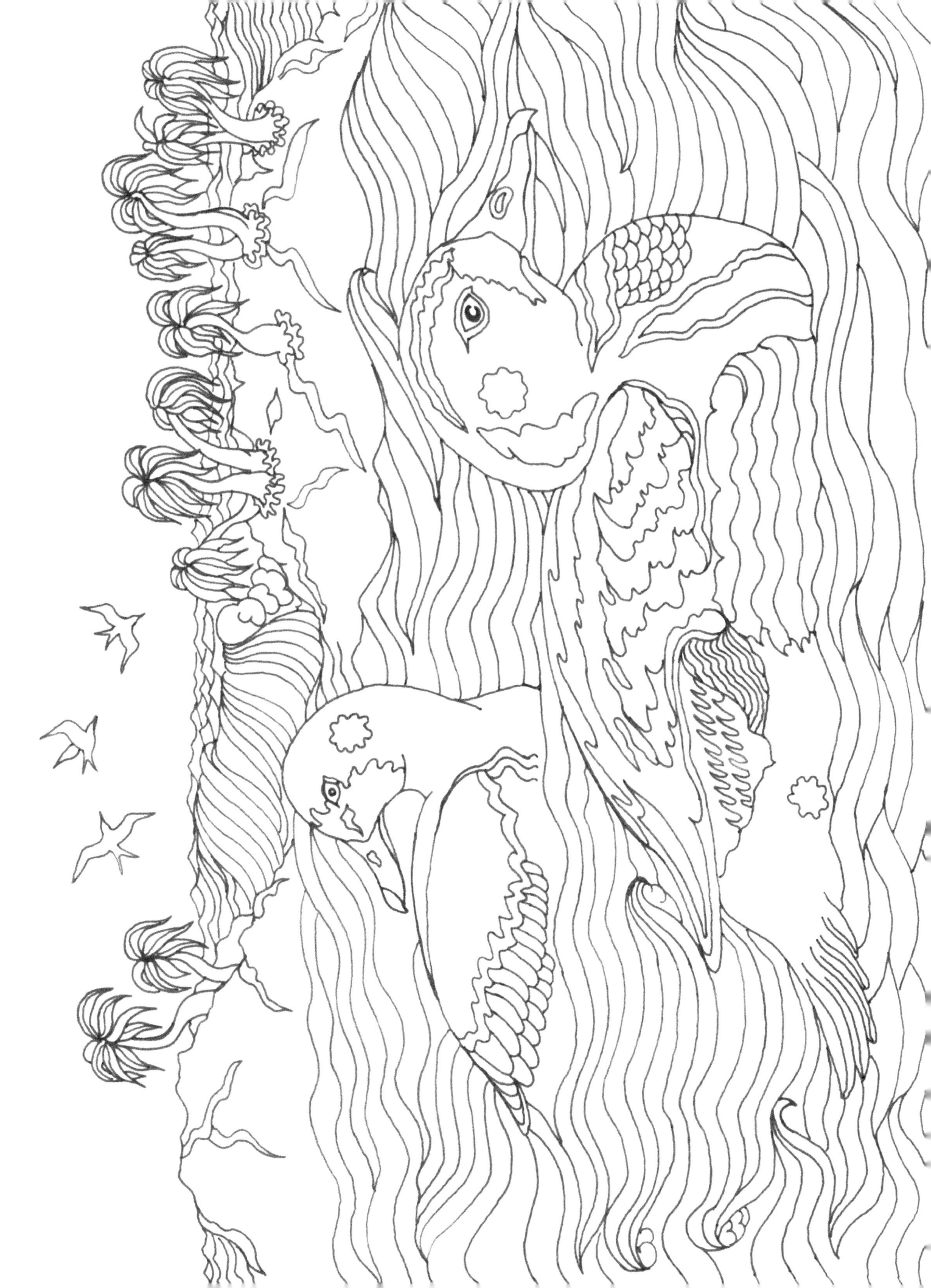

←

Harlequin duck
(Histrionicus histrionicus)

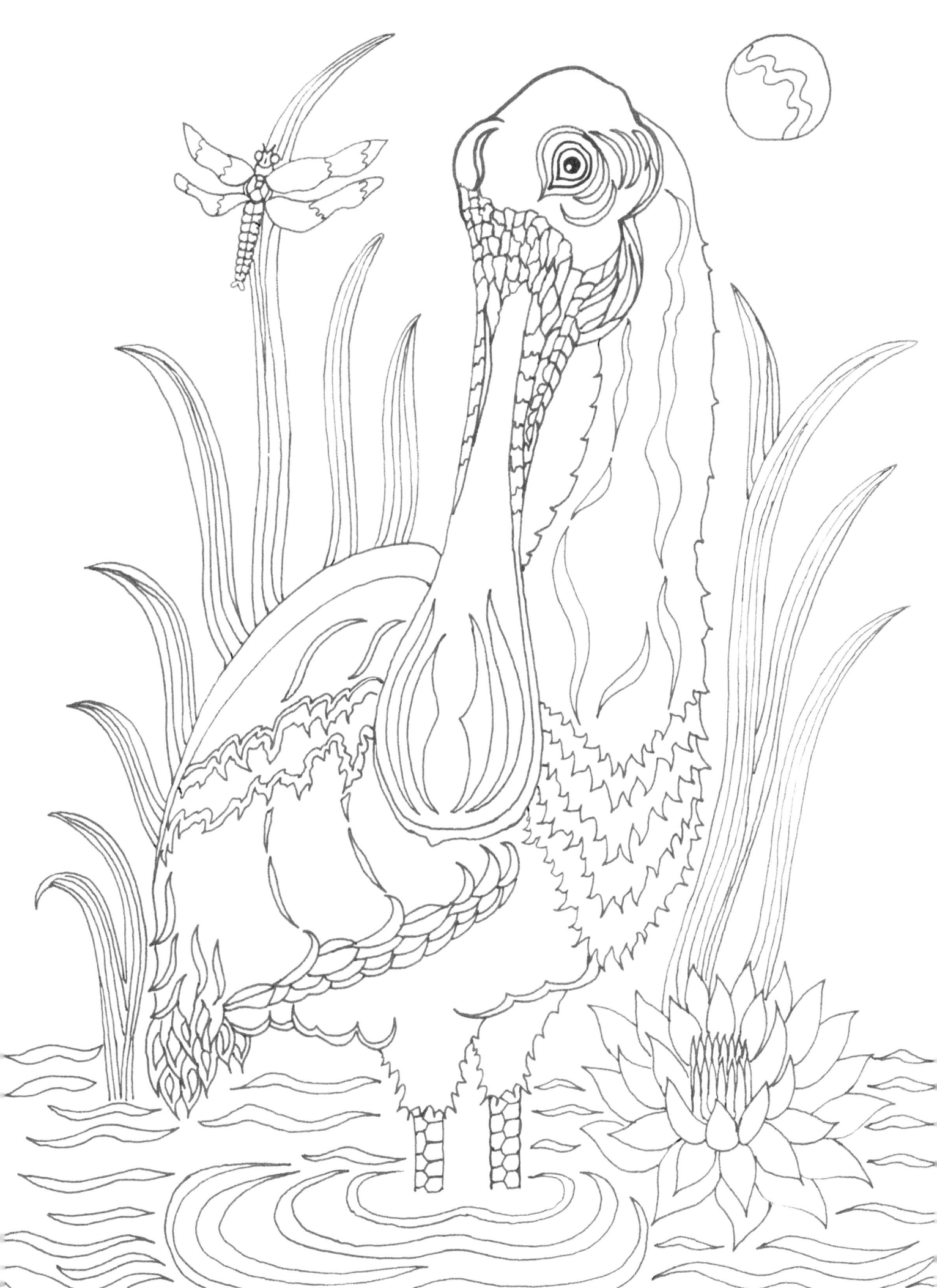

Roseate spoonbill
(*Platalea ajaja*)

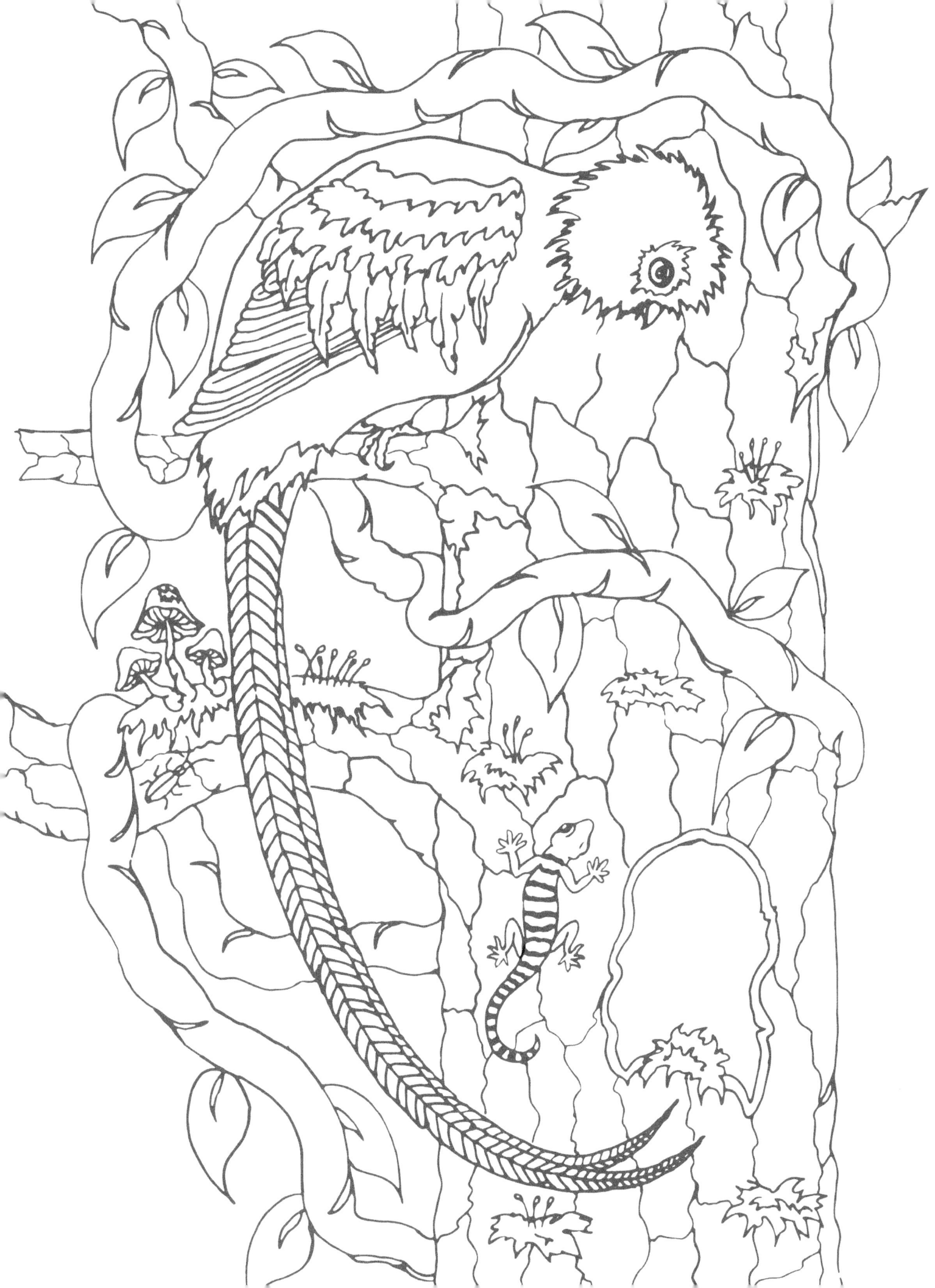

←

Resplendent quetzal
(Pharomachrus mocinno)

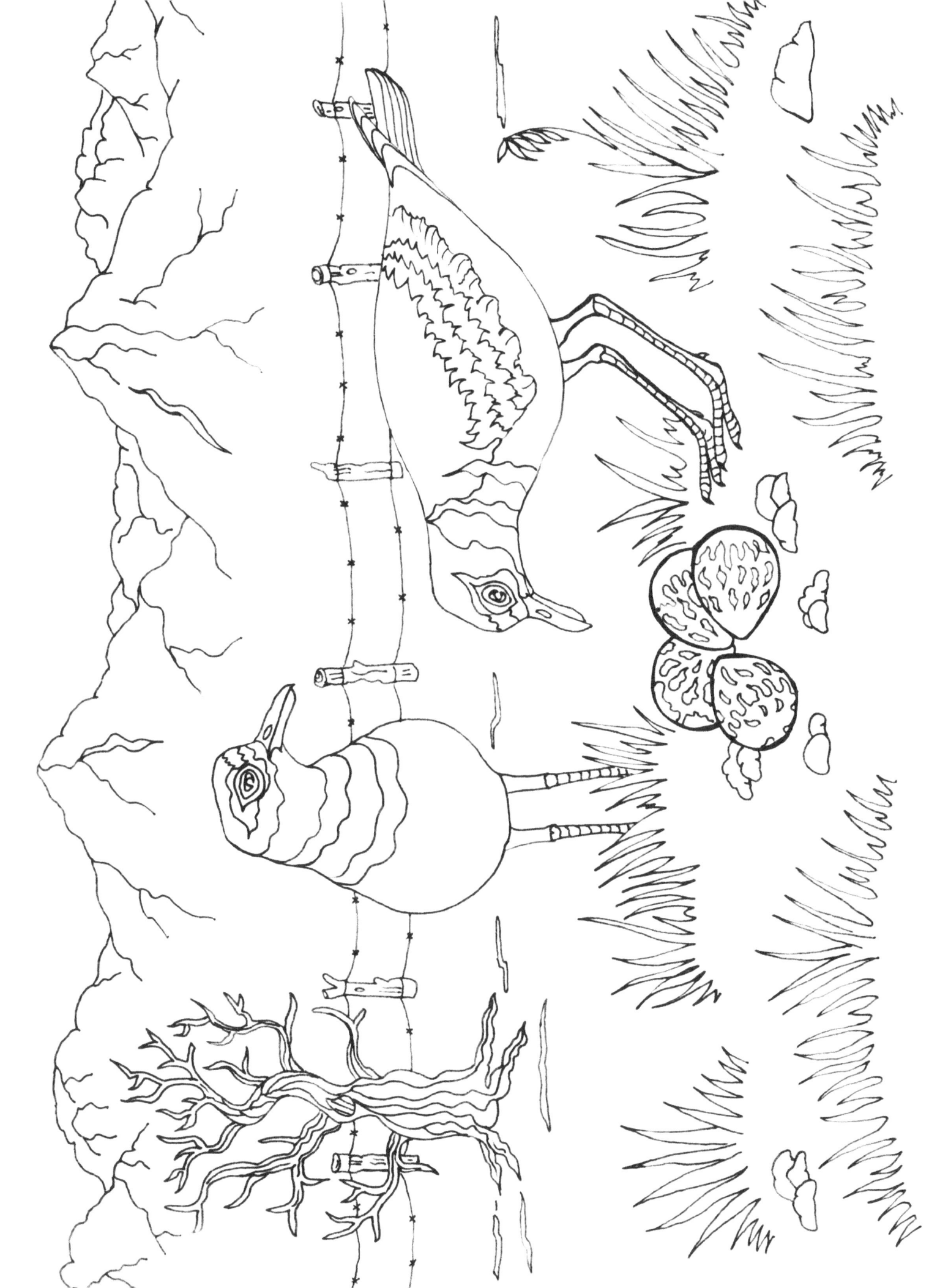

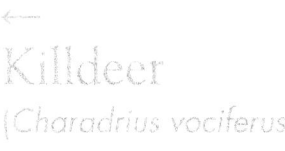

Killdeer
(*Charadrius vociferus*)

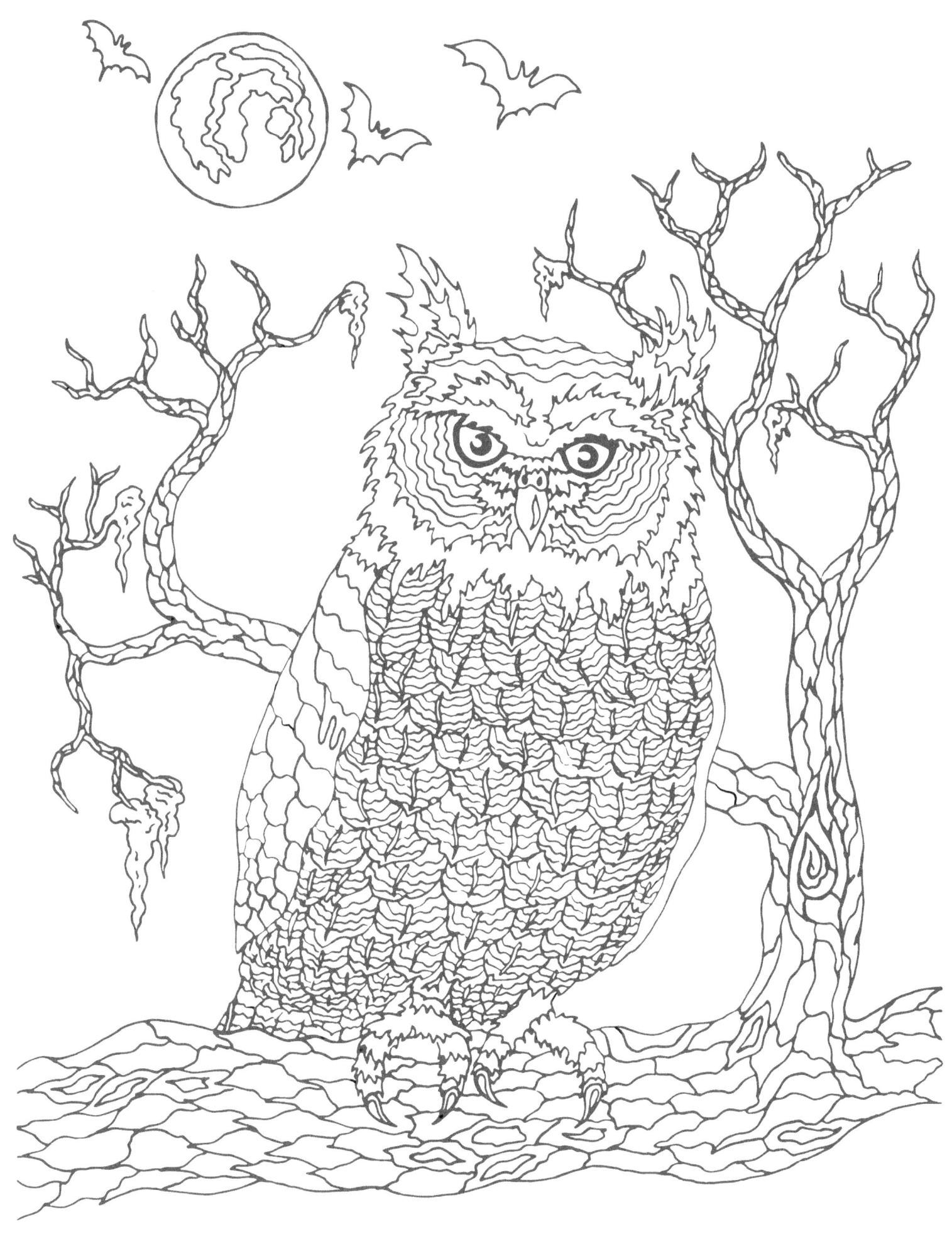

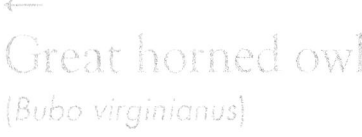

Great horned owl
(Bubo virginianus)

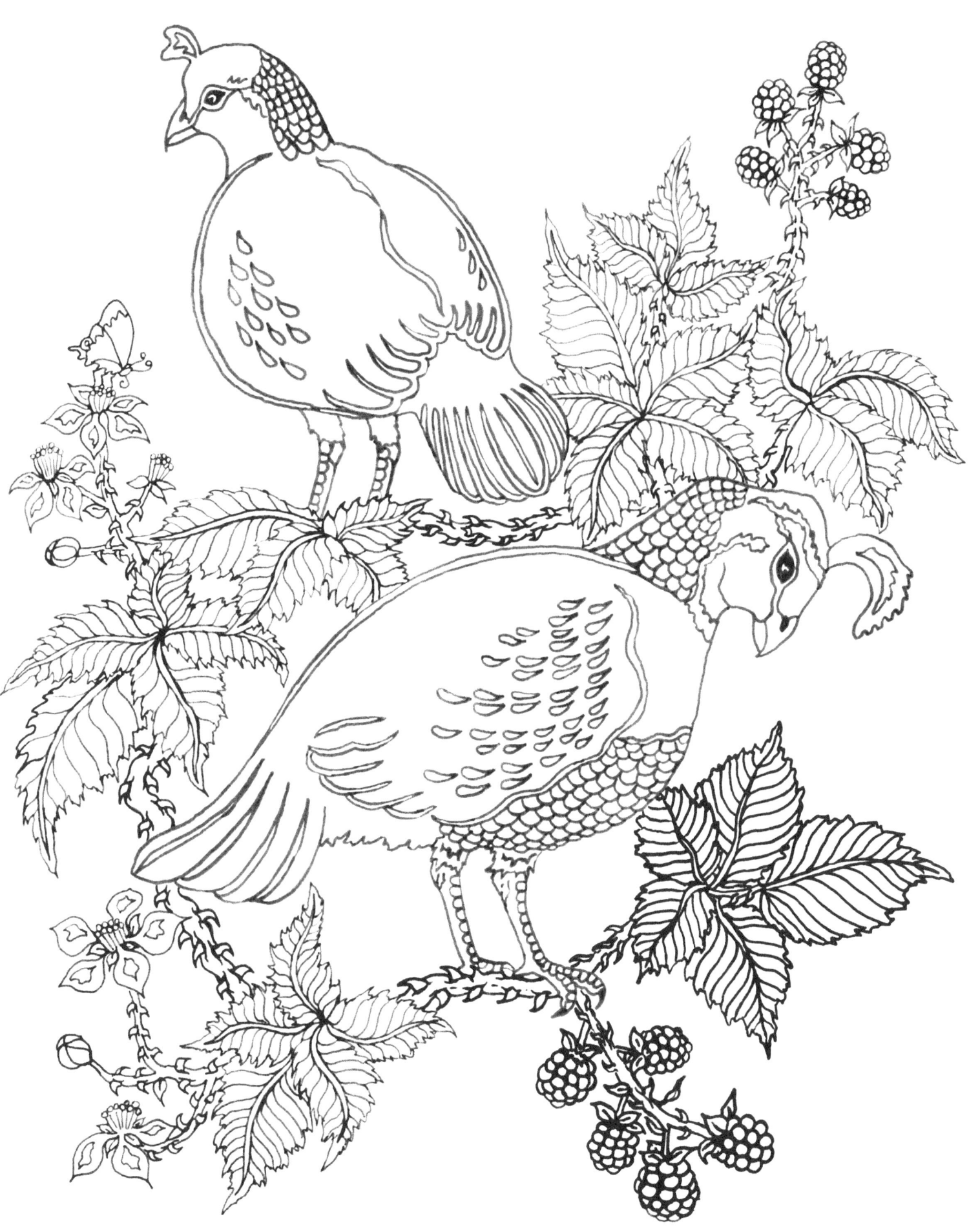

←

California quail
(*Callipepla californica*)

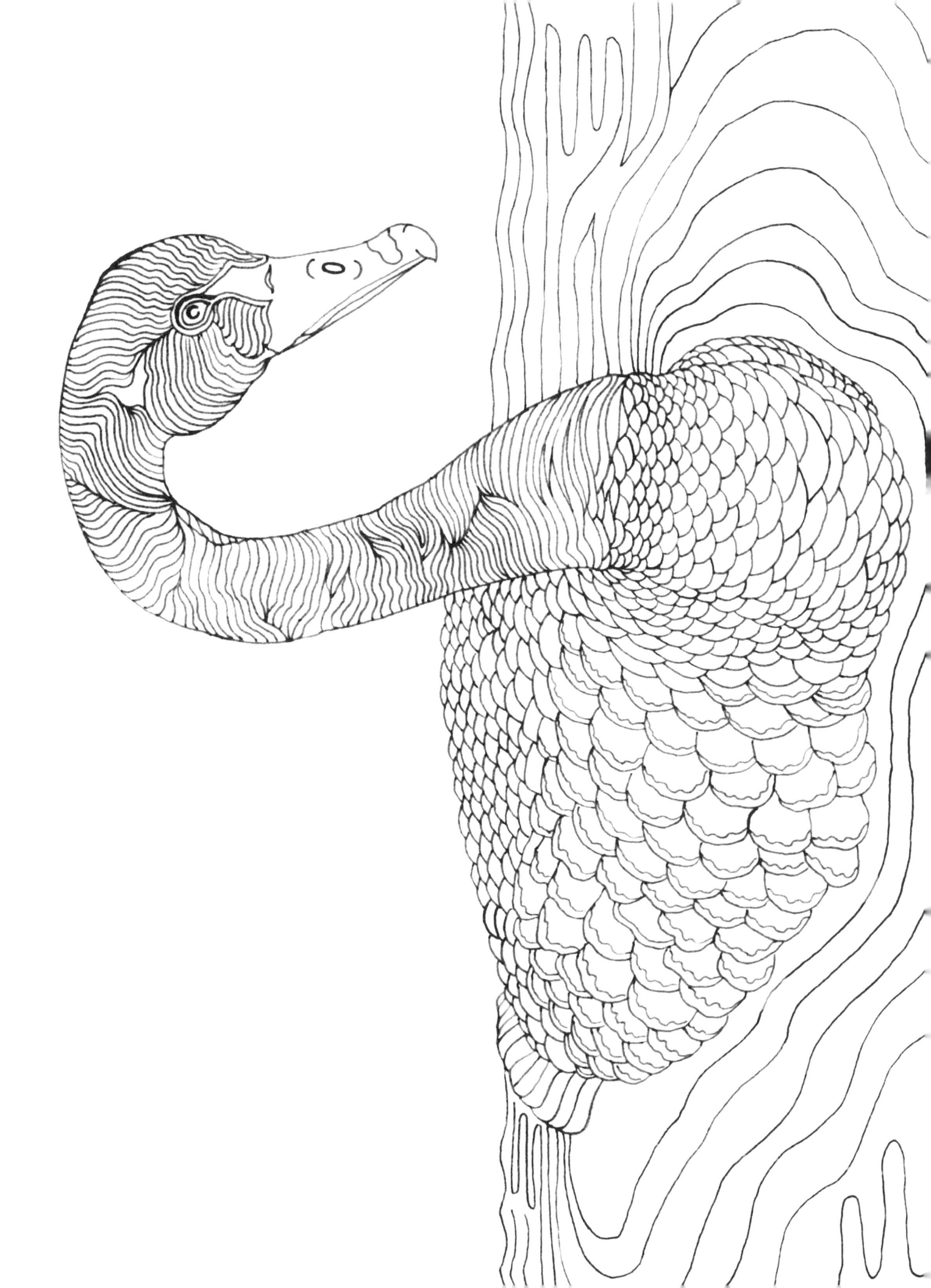

←

Black swan
(*Cygnus atratus*)

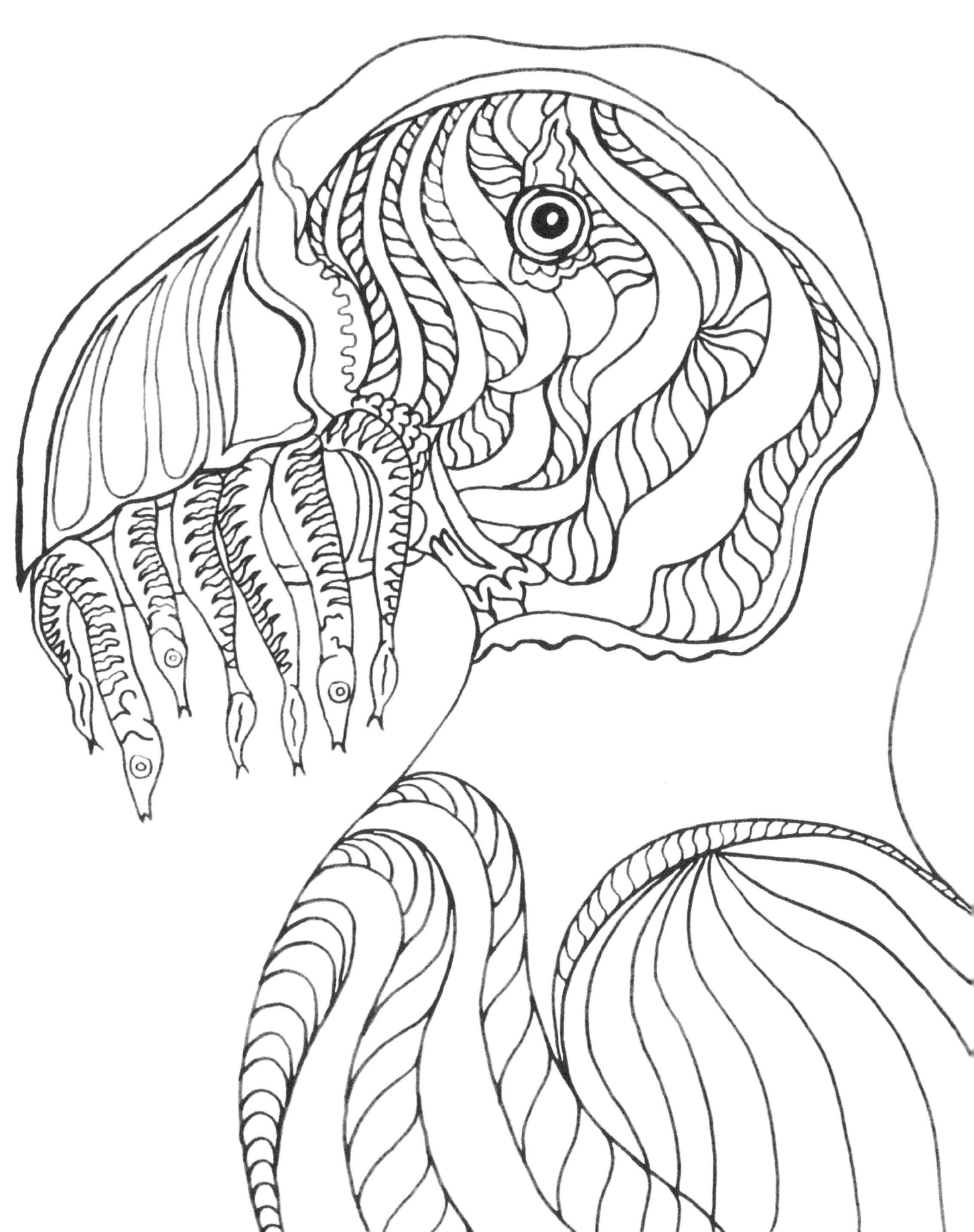

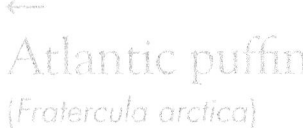

Atlantic puffin
(Fratercula arctica)

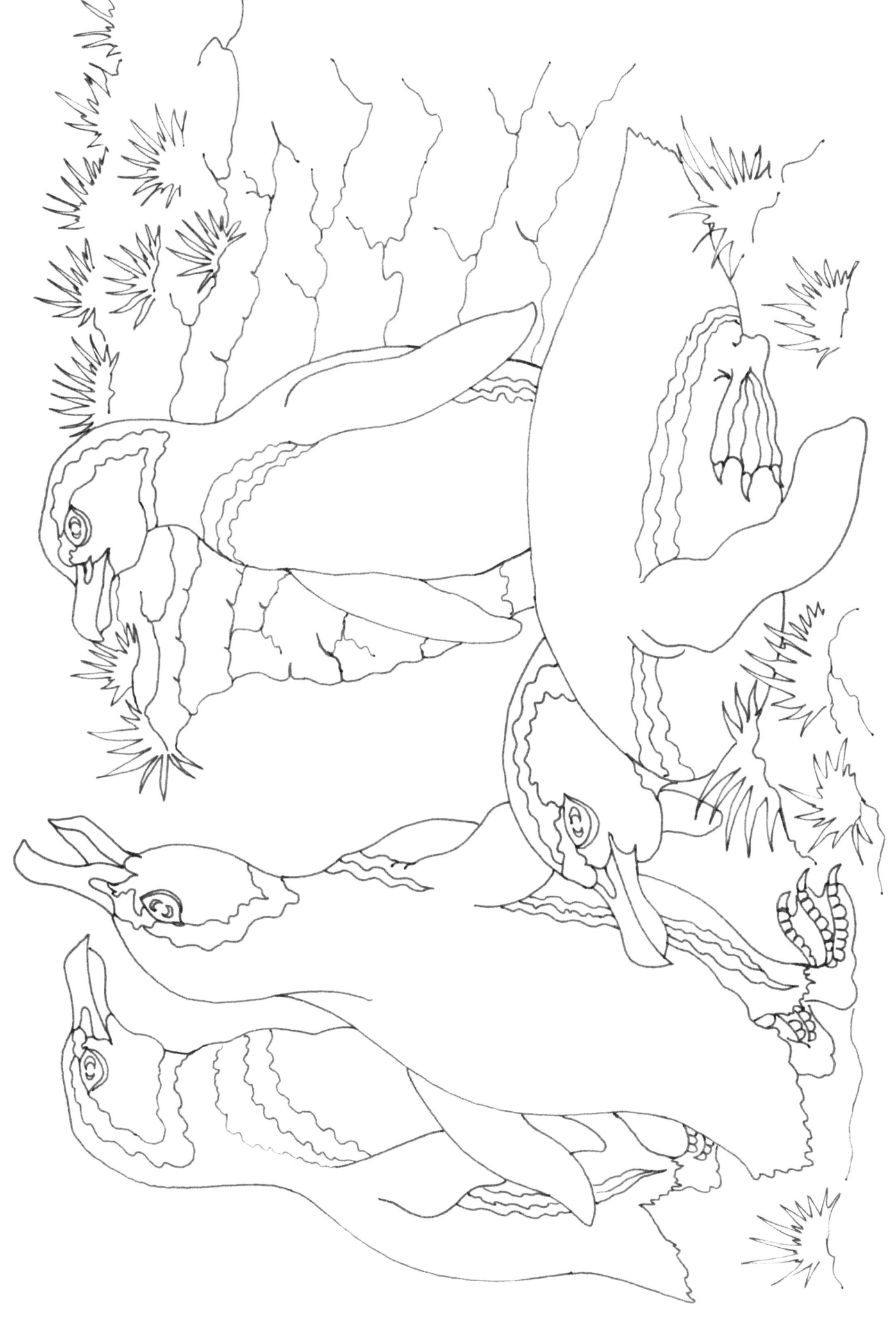

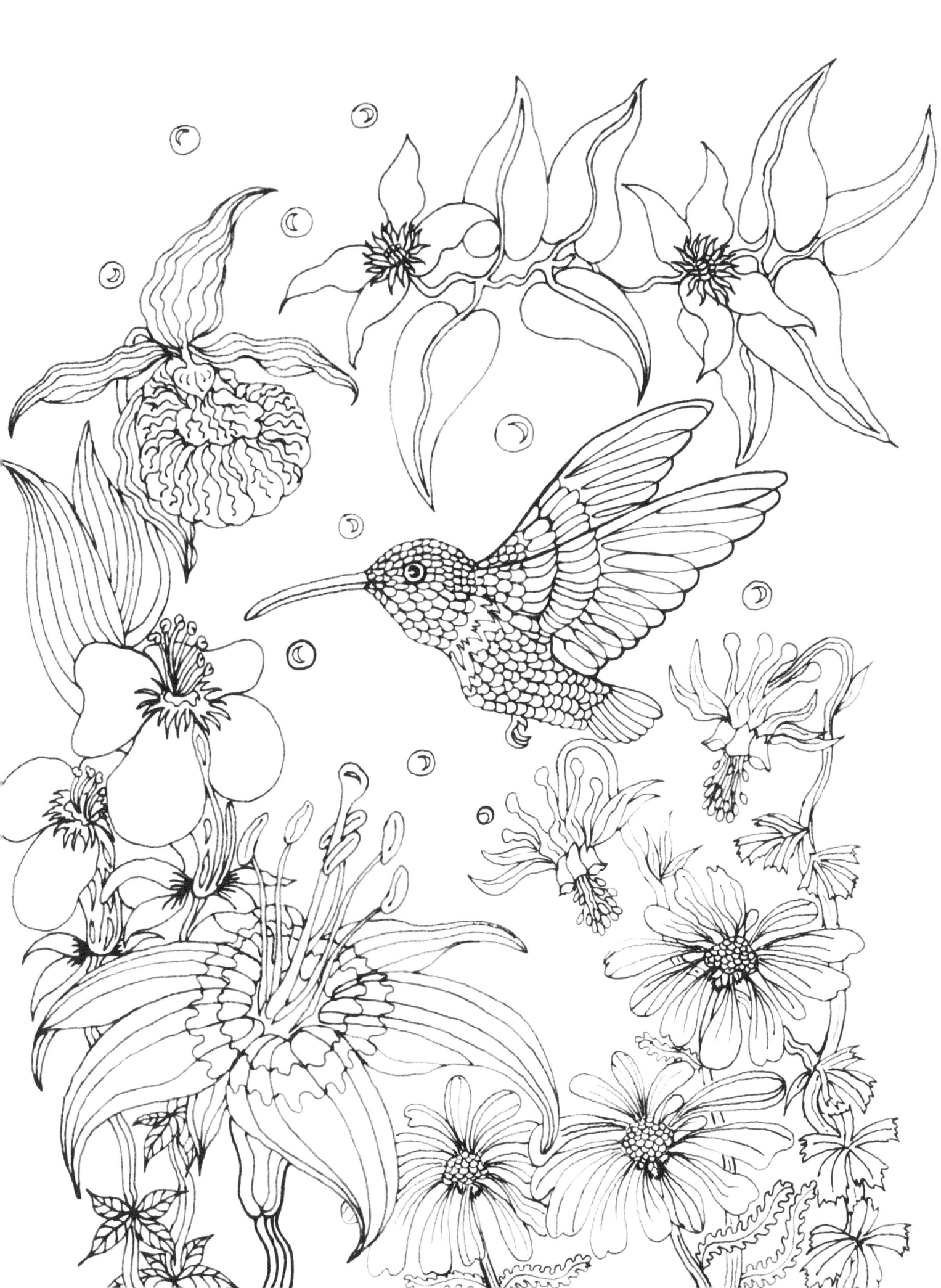

← ⋯

Rufous hummingbird
(*Selasphorus rufus*)

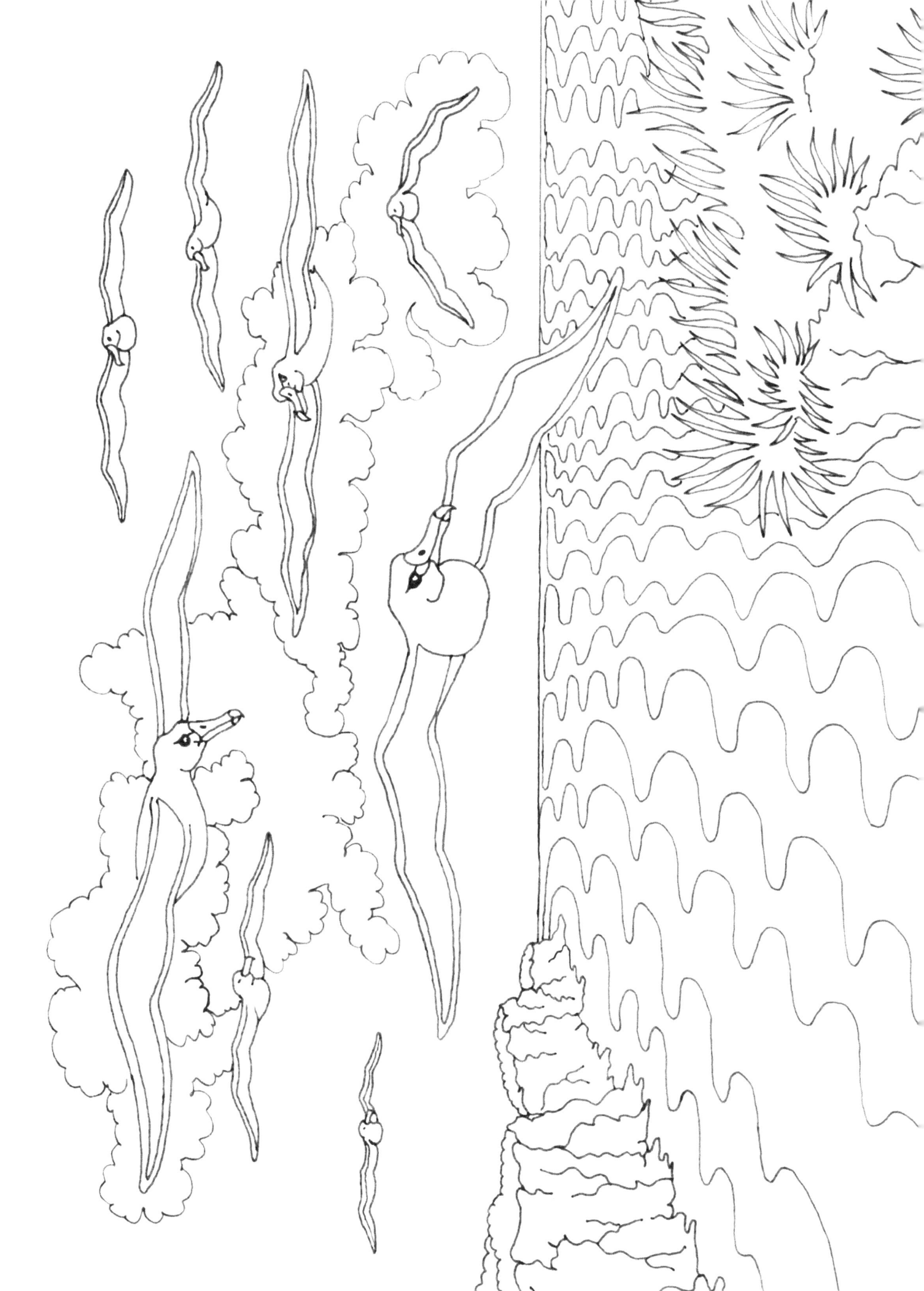

←

Laysan albatross
(Phoebastria immutabilis)

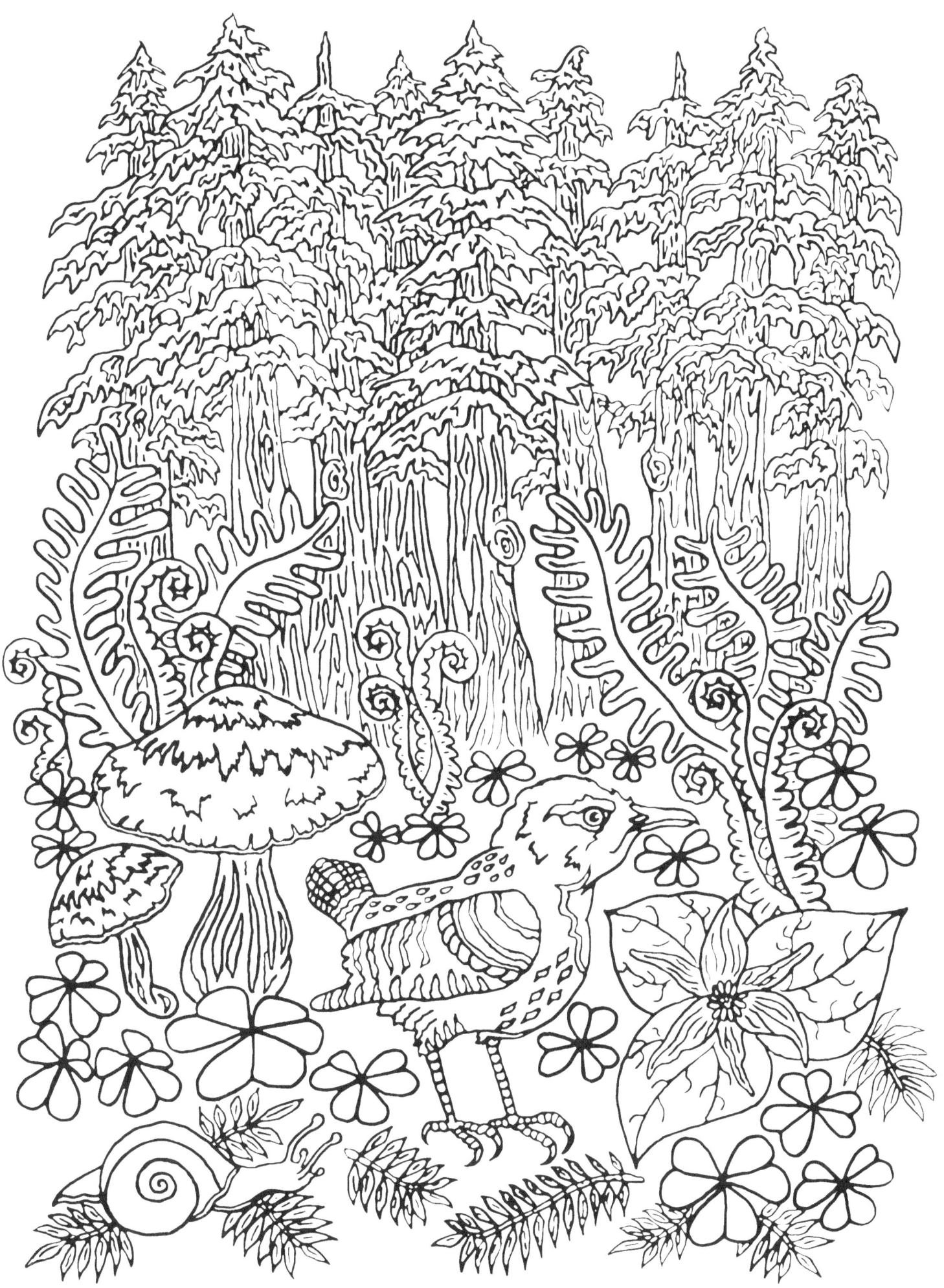

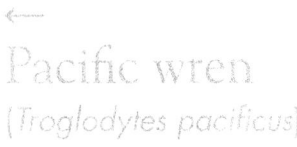

Pacific wren
(Troglodytes pacificus)

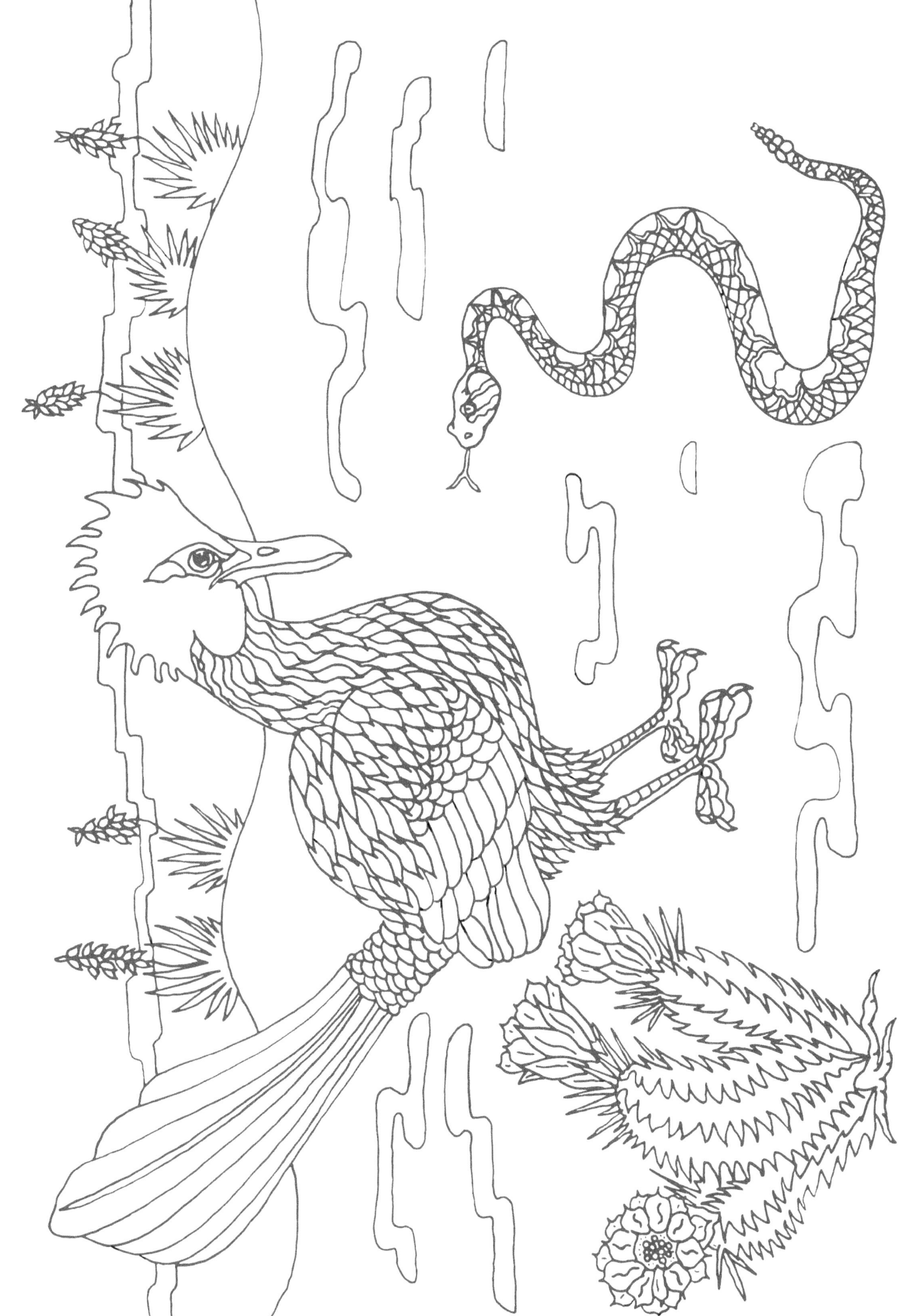

←

Greater roadrunner
(Geococcyx californianus)

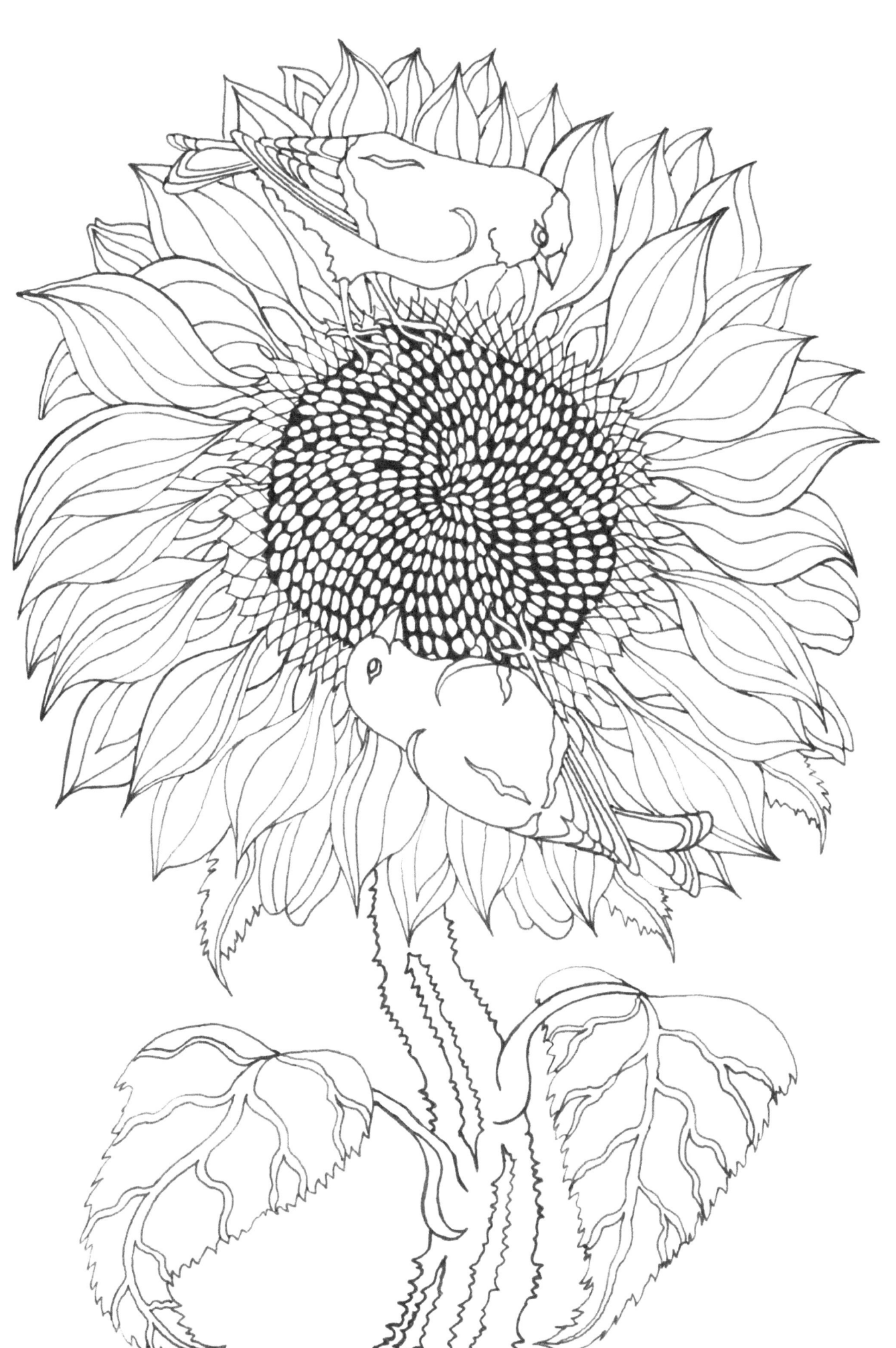

American goldfinch
(*Spinus tristis*)

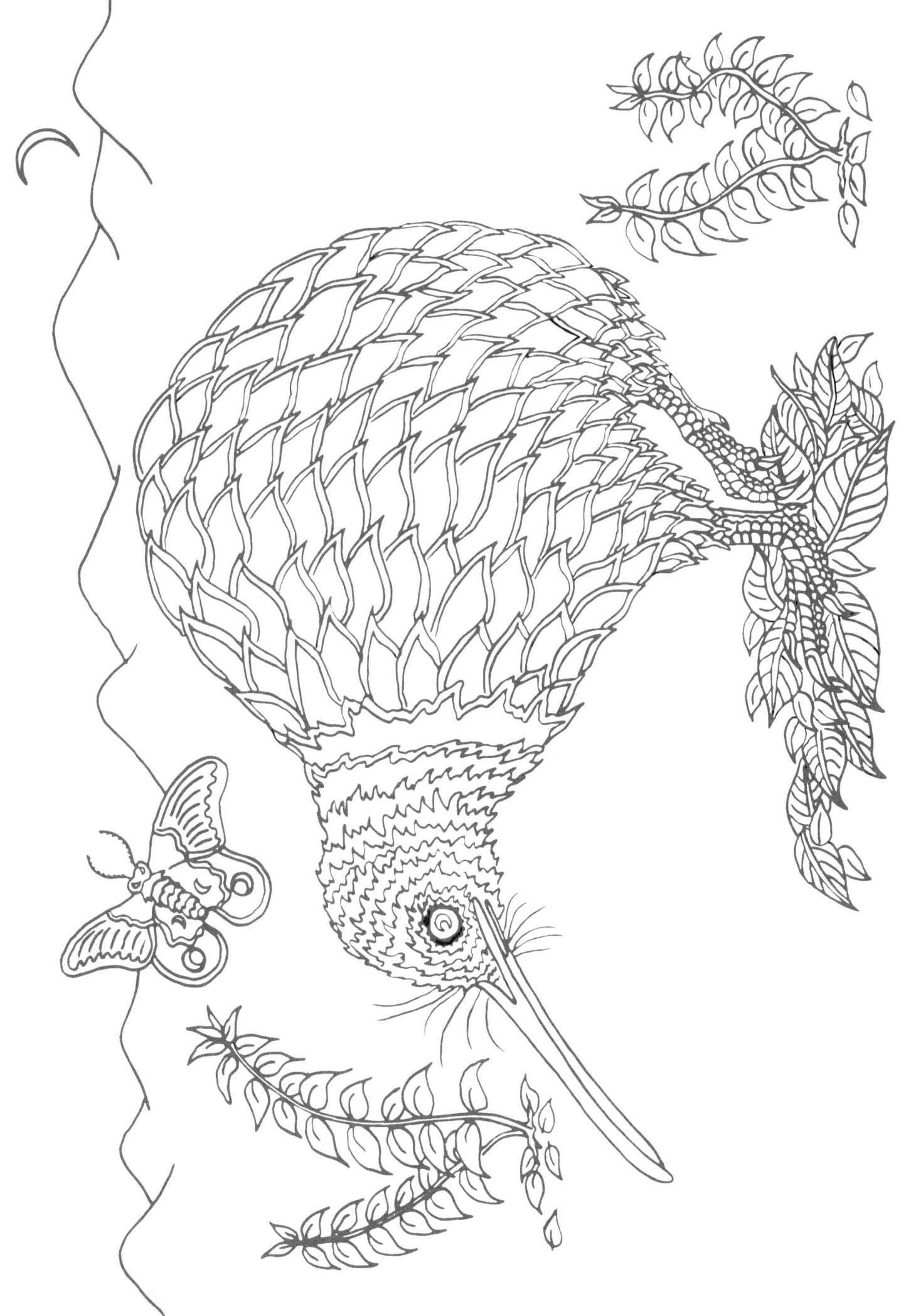

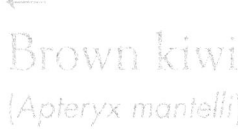

←

Brown kiwi
(Apteryx mantelli)

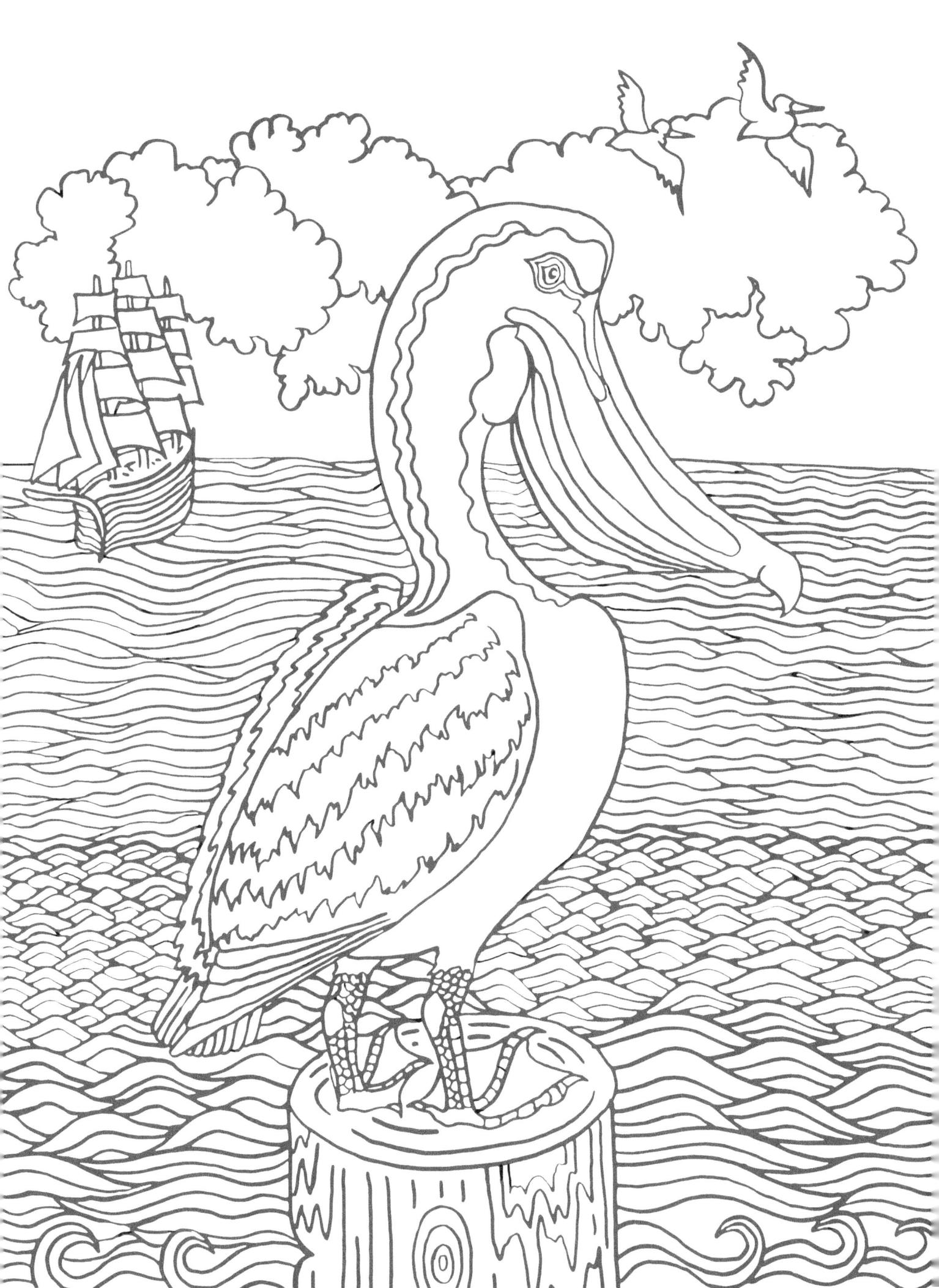

←

Brown pelican
(Pelecanus occidentalis)

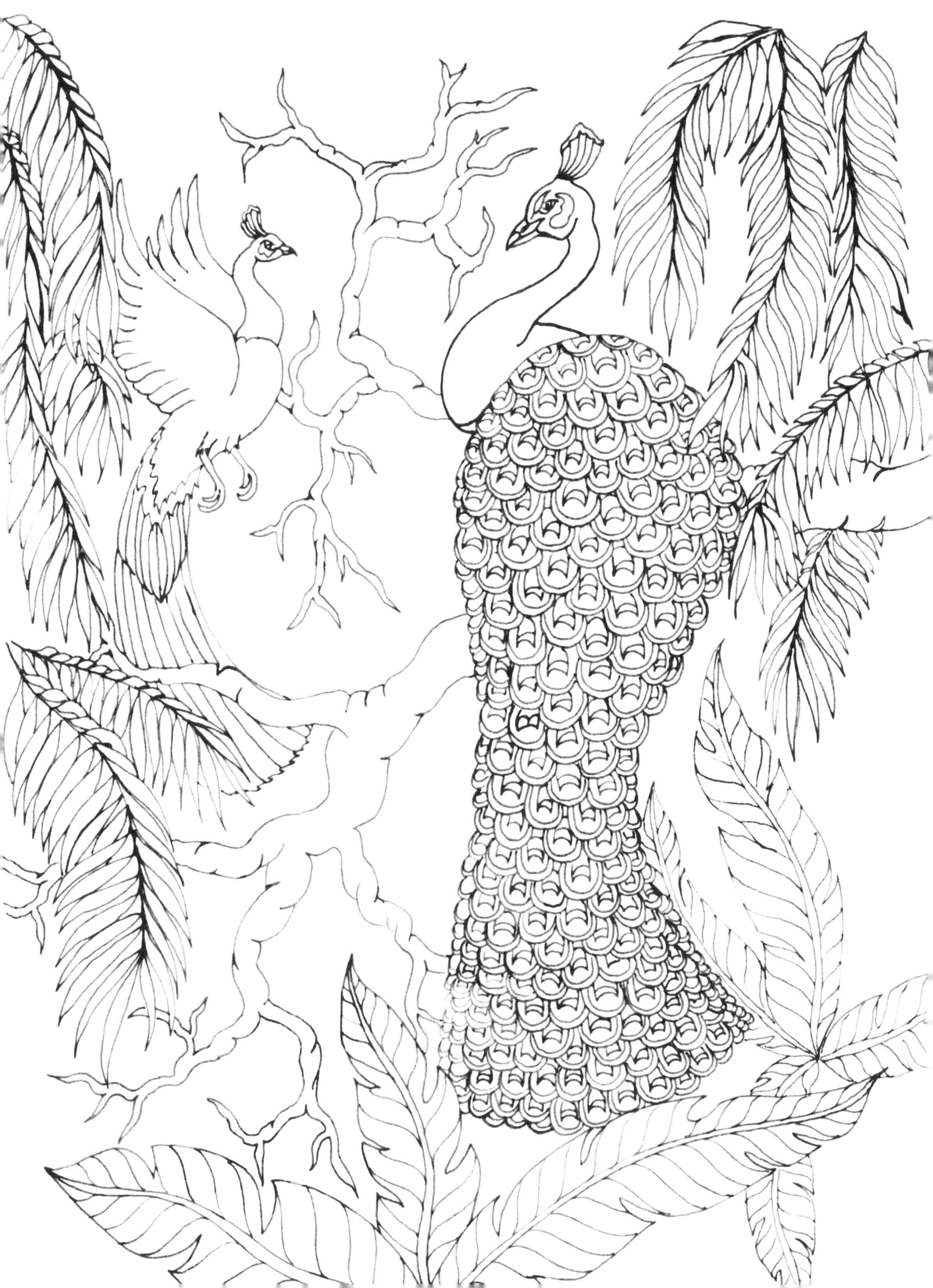

←

Indian peafowl
(*Pavo cristatus*)

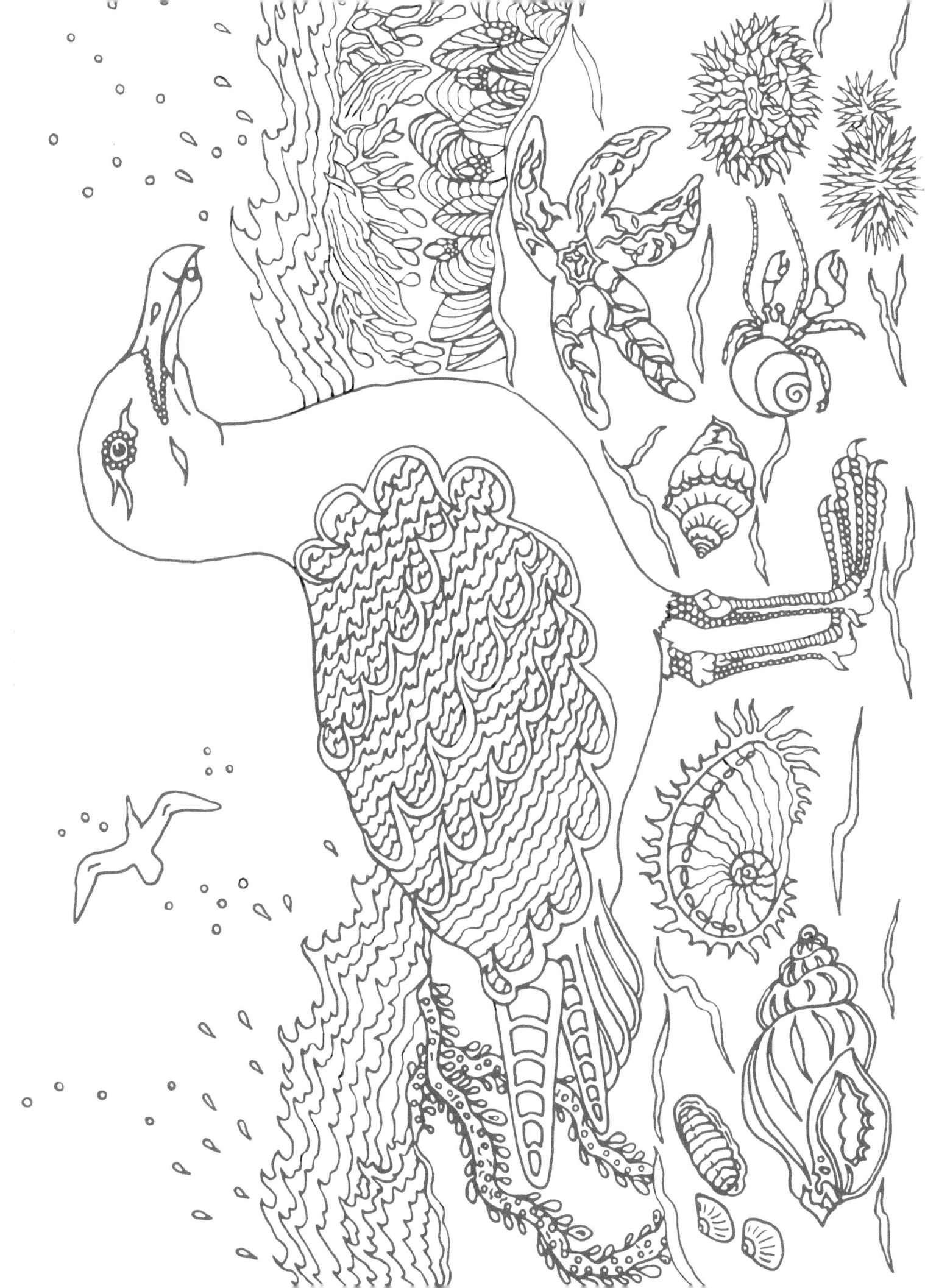

←

Western gull

(*Larus occidentalis*)

www.ingramcontent.com/pod-product-compliance
Lightning Source LLC
Chambersburg PA
CBHW080924170526
45158CB00008B/2220